W9-CKR-160

Teamwork
TRAINING

Includes CD-ROM with
Ready-to-Use Microsoft
PowerPoint™ Presentations

Exercises, Handouts, Assessments, and Tools
to Help You:
✔ Foster Effective Teamwork Competencies
at All Levels
✔ Get Buy-In and Build a Company-Wide Strategy
✔ Become a More Effective and Efficient Facilitator
✔ Ensure Training Is on Target and Gets Results

ASTD Press

Sharon Boller

ASTD Press is an internationally renowned source of insightful and practical information on workplace learning and performance topics, including training basics, evaluation and return-on-investment (ROI), instructional systems development (ISD), e-learning, leadership, and career development.

Ordering Information: Books published by ASTD Press can be purchased by visiting ASTD's website at store.astd.org or by calling 800.628.2783 or 703.683.8100.

Library of Congress Control Number: 2005922086

ISBN: 1-56286-410-6
ISSN-13: 978-1-56286-410-1

Acquisitions and Development Editor: Mark Morrow
Copyeditor: Christine Cotting, UpperCase Publication Services, Ltd.
Interior Design and Production: UpperCase Publication Services, Ltd.
Cover Design: Steve Fife
Cover Illustration: Todd Davidson

The ASTD Trainer's WorkShop Series

◆

The ASTD Trainer's WorkShop Series is designed to be a practical, hands-on road map to help you quickly develop training in key business areas. Each book in the series offers all the exercises, handouts, assessments, structured experiences, and ready-to-use presentations needed to develop effective training sessions. In addition to easy-to-use icons, each book in the series includes a companion CD-ROM with PowerPoint presentations and electronic copies of all supporting material featured in the book.

Other books in the Trainer's WorkShop Series:

- ◆ *New Supervisor Training*
  John E. Jones and Chris W. Chen

- ◆ *Customer Service Training*
  Maxine Kamin

- ◆ *New Employee Orientation Training*
  Karen Lawson

- ◆ *Leading Change Training*
  Jeffrey Russell and Linda Russell

- ◆ *Leadership Training*
  Lou Russell

- ◆ *Coaching Training*
  Chris W. Chen

- ◆ *Project Management Training*
  Bill Shackelford

- ◆ *Innovation Training*
  Ruth Ann Hattori and Joyce Wycoff

- ◆ *Sales Training*
  Jim Mikula

- ◆ *Communication Skills Training*
  Maureen Orey and Jenni Prisk

- ◆ *Strategic Planning Training*
  Jeffrey Russell and Linda Russell

- ◆ *Diversity Training*
  Cris Wildermuth, with Susan Gray

Contents

Chapter 9   HANDOUTS   133

◆

When I was invited to write this book on teamwork training, I had decisions to make: What's the right focus? Should I focus on the team leader's perspective or the team member's perspective? Should I include information on assembling a team according to individual styles? Based on my own experiences and the experiences of numerous colleagues in a variety of organizations, I quickly realized I needed a dual focus: skills associated with fostering teamwork and skills associated with demonstrating teamwork. I also recognized that few, if any, organizations really have the luxury of assembling perfect teams—ones in which a variety of learning and work styles mesh perfectly. The reality is that most people never get to figure out their learning styles; they just have to do the work. Being right-brained versus left-brained or a D versus an I is less an issue than having a basic belief in the value of teamwork.

One of my first steps in creating this book was to develop competency models for fostering teamwork and demonstrating teamwork and to find out if these models were viable. After researching competencies and assembling models, I convened two different focus groups to review these models and react to them. My groups had lots to say about the competencies and the topic of teamwork training!

People loved the competency models but reacted skeptically to the idea of teamwork training. Most people believed that teamwork is as much a philosophy as it is a skill. If you don't buy into the concept of teamwork, then no amount of training on it will convince you to demonstrate or foster it. I quickly learned that many people have had very bad experiences with teamwork training. One person literally rolled her eyes and said she didn't believe in such training.

As I questioned the groups further, I learned that people hate feeling manipulated, and they sense that many teamwork training experiences do just that—manipulate them. The activities are set up in such a way that learners are destined first to fail and then they're supposed to experience an Ah-ha! moment in which they realize they failed because they didn't operate effectively as a team. The other major complaint about such training that I heard from my groups is that most of it focuses too much on *doing* a teamwork experience and too little on *debriefing* that experience to reveal lessons learned. And it seems that teamwork training doesn't try to gauge people's attitudes about operating in a team structure and about the barriers that prevent successful teamwork.

The tools and workshops that are part of this book were shaped by these focus groups as well as by my own experience as a training designer and as both a member and a leader of teams. They are pragmatic in their goals. The "experiences" included in the workshops all serve a purpose. The debriefings that follow these activities are much more extensive than the experiences themselves. The results, I hope, are workshops that employees will see as useful and realistic rather than as fluff.

I could not have written this book and designed these workshops without the help and support of many people. First and foremost, I want to thank my husband, Kirk, who provided numerous pragmatic insights into what *team* means and exemplified teamwork to me. Thanks, too, to my two children, Steve and Beth, from whom I've learned so much regarding team versus group and "me" versus "we." I also want to thank members of the focus groups who reviewed the competency models and discussed ways to foster teamwork and teach teamwork: Chris Battell, Bill Campbell, Dave Dishong, Jan Green, Joanne Martin, Len Mozzi, Ellen Pericak, Jen Rotz, Karen Valencic, and Karen Zwick. Another thank you goes to Dawn Snyder for her excellent insights regarding teamwork competencies.

Special thanks also go to Mark Morrow, acquisitions editor for ASTD, for expressing confidence in my ability to write this book.

This book is dedicated to all who struggle to grasp the meaning and power of teams and to those who exemplify team characteristics and demonstrate the power of teamwork.

Sharon Boller
October 2005

Introduction: Who Needs Teamwork?

What's in This Chapter?

- ◆ A description of the actions involved in teamwork

- ◆ An explanation of the power of teamwork

- ◆ A discussion of factors that operate against teamwork

- ◆ An explanation of how to use this book most effectively

- ◆ A description of what's in this workbook and on the accompanying CD

You've purchased this book because you recognize the power of teamwork and you want to develop people's abilities to foster teamwork and to demonstrate teamwork. When people use teamwork, they

- ◆ listen to others' ideas in a nonjudgmental fashion and allow ideas to be expressed without "squashing" them prematurely

- ◆ offer constructive feedback to others with the goal of improving processes and outcomes

- ◆ listen to feedback and act on it when it can help a team or group improve

- ◆ share ideas, allowing them to go from "my" idea to "our" idea.

- ◆ assist others when needed

- ◆ share expertise

- ◆ work together to accomplish a task more efficiently and effectively

- ◆ trust each other.

And...when the above behaviors become routine within a group, a team, or an entire organization, the results can be amazing.

Why Teamwork Is So Powerful

Teamwork enables individuals to do together what they cannot accomplish by themselves. Examples of effective teamwork inspire us and help us see the value of teams and/or teamwork. Everyday and famous examples include the following:

- **Surgical teams.** When is the last time a heart surgeon operated alone on a patient? And if the members of the surgical team do not work together, what is the prognosis for the patient? Every day people's lives are saved or enhanced because of teamwork in operating rooms.

- **Firefighting teams.** Ever see a single firefighter put out a house fire? What would happen if the members of the firefighting team didn't talk to each other or members didn't trust their teammates to execute their responsibilities? The teamwork demonstrated by firefighters saves lives and property. This teamwork is so ingrained that the responders on the scene of a fire can execute teamwork automatically.

- **NASA's Apollo 13 mission.** One person could not have saved Apollo 13. It took the efforts of many people working together under incredible stress, both on the ground and in space, to avoid a tragedy and bring the astronauts home safely.

- **Project teams.** Groups of people bring a project to closure on time, within budget, and in alignment with required performance standards. Such teams may not have the glamour or high profile of the surgical or firefighting team, but they exemplify what great teamwork can achieve. If you've had the chance to be part of a high-functioning project team, you know how much enthusiasm, energy, and excitement such an experience can generate.

People who foster or demonstrate teamwork understand its benefits. They recognize that teamwork yields far better results than when people work in isolation or against each other. They also know that lack of teamwork can sabotage the greatest plans or the noblest task—even if several incredibly talented people are focused on the plan or the task. To put this into everyday language, no matter how talented a quarterback is, he doesn't win a football game by himself.

So, if teamwork yields such awesome results, why isn't everyone doing it?

Why Teamwork Doesn't Happen

When people in your organization fail to demonstrate teamwork, it may be because (1) they have been assigned to work on a team that isn't really a team, (2) they don't embrace the philosophy of teamwork, and/or (3) they need skill development in the teamwork competency. A brief review of each reason may help you diagnose which ones are true for your organization.

Reason 1: The team isn't really a team, but is supposed to function as one. Organizations tend to label groups of people as teams even when they lack the criteria to truly exist as such. To be a team, a group must be focused on a common task or goal. No *task* means no *team*. Too often, employees are told they are going to be part of a "team," but they aren't united by a common purpose or a need to work together to achieve results. It's tough to practice teamwork in such a setting because teamwork requires this focus on a common purpose.

Reason 2: People don't understand or embrace the teamwork philosophy. Americans love great teams and they get inspired by them, but they value individuality and personal recognition. The American workplace and social culture want teams and teamwork, but they recognize and reward individual excellence. There's no "I" in team, but there is a lot of "I" in many cultural and workplace norms. Here are a few examples that promote individuality and minimize the power of teamwork:

- *Admiration for celebrities, status, and heroes.* Even in "team" sports or movies featuring a large cast of characters, frequently the efforts of one individual take center stage. In sports and entertainment media, stories often focus on how a "star" made or ruined the movie or one player led the team to victory or defeat.

- *Ambition for individual recognition and awards.* The accomplishments of individual performers or contributors consistently receive recognition—even down to grade school and high school levels where awards go to the top achievers in various areas. In the workplace this phenomenon translates into compensation, recognition, and advancement programs based on individual achievement rather than team efforts. Individual performance still drives most incentive plans and recognition programs. When organizations begin rewarding employees for demonstrating teamwork, people will become more motivated to learn it and demonstrate it.

◆ *The proliferation of "reality" television shows.* Reality shows play on people's fascination with competition, winning, and individual rewards. The majority of these shows, which are wildly popular, pit people against each other rather than encourage collaboration for the benefit of all. Manipulation is more valued than cooperation. Collaboration may happen, but only if it benefits the individual.

Reason 3: People simply don't know how to "do" teamwork. In large part because of Reason 2, many people have never learned how to practice teamwork or foster it in others, It's not taught in schools (perhaps with the exception of MBA programs). Many teamwork behaviors—listening, offering and accepting feedback, sharing ideas, sharing expertise—are not intuitive to people. Through a host of experiences, most people are taught a "me" focus. For teamwork to flourish in organizations, employees must learn to balance this "me" focus with a "we" focus (Manz et al., 1997, p. 22).

How This Workbook Can Help Improve Teamwork

The starting point for cultivating teamwork within a team or an organization is to distinguish between two competencies—fostering teamwork and demonstrating teamwork. This workbook addresses both competencies with the assumption that people who lead teams or groups take on responsibility for fostering teamwork.

This workbook contains resources to help you address both competencies. Specifically, you will find resources and tools to

- ◆ define each competency (chapter 2)

- ◆ help your organization's employees assess their competency in fostering or demonstrating teamwork (chapter 3)

- ◆ help senior management gain buy-in to each competency on an organizationwide basis (chapter 4)

- ◆ deliver workshops for people responsible for fostering teamwork, as well as for those who need to demonstrate teamwork (chapters 5 and 6)

- help managers foster a more teamlike attitude and environment on the job (chapter 7)

- create an implementation strategy for undertaking an effort to improve teamwork throughout the organization (chapter 11).

How to Use the Contents of the Workbook and the Accompanying CD

Whether you are an experienced trainer or a novice instructor, you will find this workbook a useful resource for developing and facilitating teamwork competency workshops. By understanding the basic concepts about effective teamwork skills, and then reviewing the sample training program designs offered here, you will be able to customize the program designs for your specific audiences.

The training materials included in the book and on the accompanying CD-ROM include the following:

- Tools and strategies for assessing existing teamwork competencies— both in fostering teamwork and in demonstrating teamwork.

- Guidelines and tools for designing teamwork competency workshops.

- Instructions for facilitating your training sessions.

- Strategies and instruments for evaluating the learning.

- Training workshop sample agendas that incorporate a range of training activities. The agendas can be used "as is" or modified to suit your organization, its challenges, and your own teaching style.

- Microsoft PowerPoint presentations you can use to focus the attention of workshop participants on the content of the program. Thumbnail versions of all of the slides appear at the ends of the chapters in which they are used. The CD also contains black-and-white versions of the slides that can be printed on paper and used as handouts or printed on film and used as overhead masters.

The CD also contains printable versions (PDFs) of the assessments, handouts, tools, and training instruments provided in this workbook. Follow the instructions in the appendix, "Using the Compact Disc," at the back of the workbook or read "How to Use This CD.doc" on the CD.

Icons

For easy reference, icons are included in the margins of this book to help you quickly locate materials and tools or make key instructional points during a workshop. Here is what the icons look like and what they indicate:

 Assessment: Appears when an agenda or learning activity includes an assessment.

 CD: Indicates materials included on the CD accompanying this workbook.

 Clock: Indicates suggested timeframes for an activity.

 Discussion Question: Points out questions you can use to set up or debrief a workshop learning activity or a team-building activity.

 Handout: Indicates handouts you can print or copy to enhance the experience during a workshop or a team-building activity.

 **Key Point:** Alerts you to key points to emphasize during either a workshop or a team-building exercise, or points out special information for the instructor.

 **Learning Activity:** Identifies learning activities that are part of the workshops in chapters 4 through 6.

 PowerPoint item: Indicates PowerPoint presentations and slides that can be used individually.

 Tool: Identifies tools that are used before, during, or after training workshops.

 Training Instrument: Indicates interactive learning materials.

What to Do Next: Identifies actions to take after completing a section of the workbook or after completing a section of a workshop.

What to Do Next

- Skim through the contents of the entire workbook to familiarize yourself with the materials and resources contained in each chapter.

- Review chapter 2 to ensure that you understand the difference between *team* and *teamwork,* and the competencies associated with "fostering teamwork" and "demonstrating teamwork."

- Assess the competencies of individuals, teams, and the organization, depending on your area of focus (chapter 3).

- Develop an implementation strategy for addressing needs, using resources in chapter 11.

- Deliver desired workshops (chapters 4 through 6) and/or provide managers with resources to help foster teamwork within work groups and teams (chapter 7).

◆ ◆ ◆

The next chapter introduces you to two competency models: one for fostering teamwork and one for demonstrating teamwork. These two competencies are required for teamwork to occur within an organization. Consequently, they serve as the foundation for the assessments and the workshops that make up the majority of the book.

Chapter 2

Defining the Teamwork Competency

What's in This Chapter?

- ♦ Definitions of key concepts and terms

- ♦ Comprehensive lists of the behaviors required for fostering and for demonstrating teamwork

- ♦ A discussion of the possible organizational outcomes of effective teamwork

Teams and teamwork are closely linked concepts. As you get ready to develop teamwork within your organization or within teams that are part of your organization, having a clear definition of each concept is helpful. As you may have seen, many people who are part of "official" teams don't practice teamwork. And an equal number of people who work within an organization but not as part of an official team nonetheless demonstrate teamwork. In brief, a team is a group of people united around a common task. Teamwork encompasses the behaviors that help the team do its task successfully. A look at each concept in more depth is helpful.

What Is a Team?

A *team* is a group of people who are united to achieve a common goal that is too large in scope to be achieved by a single individual—or at least not efficiently achieved. Within a team, each member has a role to fulfill, and the roles are interdependent. As stated in chapter 1, what makes a group a team is the focus on a common task or goal. The bottom line: If there is no task, there is no team. Although many teams flounder because team members can't get along, an equal or greater number of teams flounder or fail because they have no common task or goal.

The definition of *team* can be expanded to include three different types of teams (Larson and LaFasto, 1989):

1. creative

2. problem-resolution

3. tactical.

It's helpful if you label the various types of teams in your organization because the elements of "teamwork" that are most critical for each type of team differ. Consequently, the emphasis of your teamwork training may need to be adjusted to accommodate the team's specific needs.

Creative teams design something, such as a new product, a new process, or a new marketing campaign. Teamwork training for creative teams needs to emphasize the importance of supporting new ideas and avoiding "idea squashing." Negativity, premature judgments, and hasty decision making can all sabotage creative teams.

Problem-resolution teams, as the name implies, solve problems. Such teams may be permanent or ad hoc. For example, your organization may assemble an ad hoc team to handle a public relations crisis or to figure out the cause of a business disaster. Other organizations (for example, the Centers for Disease Control or the Federal Aviation Administration) may have permanent team structures in place to respond to crises such as an epidemic or a plane crash. Depending on where the epidemic breaks out or the crash occurs, different team members are mobilized to study the problem, identify the cause, and when appropriate, propose a solution. In either permanent or ad hoc structures, trust is a critical component of teamwork. Team members in these types of teams work very cooperatively, with each team member relying on the other members' expertise to help build a total picture of the problem and its causes. In addition to focusing on building trust, teamwork training must help members recognize and avoid "group think." Problem-resolution teams can feel great pressure to find the cause of a problem and to propose a solution.

Tactical teams execute plans—to launch a new product, to perform a service, to produce a deliverable. Their teamwork training must emphasize goal and role clarity. Members who do not fully embrace and understand the team goal, their roles, and the roles of their teammates make it difficult for the team to succeed.

Table 2–1 offers a summary of these three team types and the team-building behaviors most important to each type.

Table 2-1

Team Types and Their Critical Team-Building Elements

TEAM TYPE	DESCRIPTION	KEY TEAM-BUILDING ELEMENTS
Creative	Designs something new	Idea sharing Idea support Idea expansion
Problem-resolution	Figures out causes of a problem Identifies solutions	Trust Cooperation
Tactical	Executes plans to produce something	Clarification of team goal(s) Clarification of member roles and responsibilities

What Is Teamwork?

Teamwork is an action—it's something people *do*. It can be demonstrated either in a group or in a team. Like teams, it requires a common focus or goal. People don't demonstrate teamwork "just because." They do it because they share a goal, mission, or vision. Actions that are labeled as *teamwork* include

- providing assistance to others when they need it

- acknowledging the efforts of others

- sharing expertise with others

- providing information, assistance, or various types of support to others in an effort to build relationships and enhance communication

- providing positive, constructive feedback to others in an effort to improve processes or outcomes

- listening to feedback offered by others and adjusting behavior accordingly

- working toward solutions that the entire group or team can support rather than focusing on solutions that offer the greatest personal benefit

- sharing ideas

- ◆ listening in a nonjudgmental way to the ideas of others

- ◆ demonstrating trust in others' abilities and ideas.

Assuming a common goal does exist and a formal team is in place, team members need competency in *demonstrating* teamwork, and a team leader needs competency in *fostering* teamwork. Teams that lack teamwork find it hard to be successful—even if all the members agree on a common goal or vision. For teams to be successful, team leaders must know how to encourage and nurture teamwork. Team members must learn how to practice teamwork.

If no formal team structures are in place, but the organization values teamwork, then a common goal must be defined that all members of a group can embrace—perhaps being the premier healthcare provider, achieving the best customer satisfaction rating in the industry, or earning the Malcolm Baldrige National Quality Award. Teamwork behaviors must then be promoted throughout the group or organization *with the goal of achieving this common purpose.*

With only a few minutes of thought, you can identify opportunities in your organization where teamwork can help improve efficiency, decrease problems, and enhance overall accountability. Here are a few workplace scenario examples in which a teamwork philosophy can pay off for a department and/or an entire organization:

- ◆ *A customer calls in with a question:* The attitude of the person taking the call can either be, "I don't have an answer so it isn't my problem. I'll just forward the call to someone else," or "We are all responsible for satisfying customers. Therefore, it's my responsibility to ensure this customer is satisfied. I'll do whatever legwork is needed to find the answer to this customer's question." This legwork may require talking to people in other departments to locate the needed information.

- ◆ *A sales rep calls to check on the status of a delivery:* The attitude of the employee in shipping who answers the call can either be, "We've got boxes stacked up to the rafters here. If he wants to know what happened to his order, he can come look for it," or "Customer satisfaction is what counts here. The loss of the order doesn't just affect the sales rep (who indeed may have contributed to the order snafu). It's important for us to make this sale and keep the customer happy. I need to locate the order and work with the rep to expedite things."

- *An IT person responds to a computer question following a new system roll-out—the same question 20 other people in the claims department have asked:* If the IT worker sees her role as helping the organization efficiently respond to customers, then she may decide to escalate the problem so it can be globally addressed. If the IT worker sees her role as simply answering questions, then she is likely to address the question and then wait for the next person to call with the same question.

- *A customer waits for service in a restaurant:* Ever been in a restaurant where no one seems to be assigned to wait on your table? When servers get focused on taking care of "their" tables, they may not notice the customer who doesn't get service. When servers are focused on making sure everyone in their field of view appears to be receiving good service, they can either acknowledge the customer themselves or make sure they alert the appropriate server to the waiting customer.

In short, an attitude of teamwork can make a difference in every organization, both inside and outside of formalized team structures. As I stated in chapter 1, the starting point for cultivating teamwork within your organization is to distinguish between two competencies—fostering teamwork and demonstrating teamwork. People who lead teams or groups assume responsibility for fostering teamwork. People who are members of a group or team must demonstrate teamwork. Tables 2–2 and 2–3 define these competencies and identify the behaviors required for each. Both models are derived from interviews with a wide range of employees, observation of teams, and extensive readings on the topics of teamwork, team leadership, and teams.

Results to Look For

When leaders effectively foster teamwork and employees consistently demonstrate teamwork, you can expect the following organizational results:

- enhanced communication flow

- increased efficiency in team efforts, work processes, and work outputs

- enhanced creativity, which can lead to innovations that improve processes, products, and services

- fewer internal and external customer complaints

- greater employee and customer satisfaction.

Table 2–2

A Competency Model for Fostering Teamwork

COMPETENCY DEFINITION	KEY BEHAVIORS

The ability to encourage and enable others to work cooperatively and/or collaboratively toward a goal	◆ Promote and gain buy-in and agreement on a common mission and goal
	◆ Reinforce the team mission or goal on an ongoing basis
	◆ Clarify roles, responsibilities, and accountabilities
	◆ Promote cooperation with other work groups or units
	◆ Establish and implement a communication framework
	◆ Create an environment that reinforces teamwork
	◆ Structure rewards and incentives to reinforce collaboration:
	  ◆ create an atmosphere that encourages collaboration instead of competition
	  ◆ provide opportunities for people to learn how to work together
	  ◆ cultivate trust among team members.
	◆ Identify and remove roadblocks that cannot be handled at the team level
	◆ Recognize the behaviors that contribute to teamwork, and coach the team and individuals within the team on these behaviors
	◆ Establish and implement team decision-making and problem-solving processes

What to Do Next

◆ Begin thinking about how significant an emphasis you want to place on the competency of teamwork within your organization. Is it something you want to develop within a single team or is it something you want to address organizationwide?

◆ Review the assessment advice and tools provided in the next chapter. Use these tools to collect data about how individuals, teams, and the organization currently rate on teamwork competencies and plot your strategy for developing teamwork inside your organization.

Table 2-3

A Competency Model for Demonstrating Teamwork

COMPETENCY DEFINITION	KEY BEHAVIORS
The ability to work cooperatively and/or collaboratively with others in pursuit of a common goal	◆ Listen and respond constructively to other group or team members' ideas ◆ Share one's own ideas with the group ◆ Openly express any concerns to other team or group members ◆ Openly express any concerns to other team or group ◆ Acknowledge when conflict exists and express disagreement constructively ◆ Give honest and constructive feedback to other team members ◆ Assist other team members, group members, or work units when needed ◆ Work toward solutions that all members of the team or group can support; support team or group decisions ◆ Share professional expertise with others

◆ ◆ ◆

Chapter 3 looks at assessing the organization's existing teamwork competencies. The tools provided there make an effective transition to the various workshops included in later chapters.

Assessing the Organizational Competency

- An explanation of the purposes of assessment in your organization

- Steps for assessing your organization's need for training in teamwork, and the right questions to ask

- Information on what data-gathering methods to use in specific circumstances and with particular groups

Before delivering any training on teamwork, your first step is to find out what's currently going on within your organization. You need to assess how well people currently practice teamwork and what results they achieve from doing so. You can then compare these data to desired performance and results. The gap between the two becomes the opportunity for performance improvement. Figure 3–1 illustrates this gap analysis.

The key is to focus not just on current and desired *behavior,* but also on current and desired *results.* Competence, after all, isn't measured by behavior; it's measured by outcomes. For example,

- if your organization labeled someone an excellent salesperson, would it be because he or she executed all steps of the sales model wonderfully or because he or she produced a lot of sales?

- if you consider someone an excellent mechanic, is your decision based on her or his appearance, demeanor, knowledge, and tools? Or is it based on the fact that she or he always fixes your car problems the first time?

Behavior is only meaningful if it produces the results you want. So as you assess how well people foster or demonstrate teamwork, you need to look at the kind of results teamwork produces and compare them with the kind of results

17

Figure 3–1

Illustration of a Performance Gap

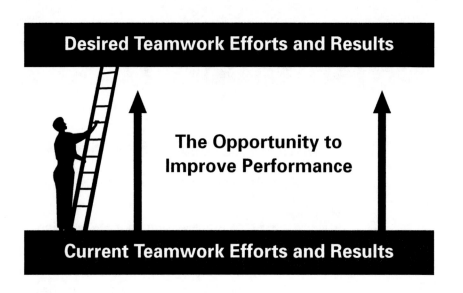

it needs to produce. The required results should stem from the business goals of the team, the department, the division, or the entire organization. Here are some examples of results that teamwork may be expected to produce. All are measurable.

On a project team,

- ◆ deliverables are produced on time, within budget, and to specified quality standards

- ◆ internal team satisfaction ratings are consistently high

- ◆ decisions are made and conflicts are resolved without escalating them outside of the team.

Within a department,

- ◆ production goals are consistently achieved

- ◆ internal employee satisfaction ratings are consistently high

- ◆ there are high internal customer satisfaction ratings from other departments, regardless of whether the interaction was a one-time incident or a routine part of doing business

- ◆ there are high satisfaction ratings from external customers.

On an organizationwide level,

◆ internal and external customer complaints are reduced

◆ production increases

◆ processing times are reduced

◆ customer satisfaction ratings or industry ratings increase.

Reviewing one example of the effect that teamwork within a service department has on customer satisfaction ratings may help clarify this point. A local Honda dealership has received numerous awards from Honda Motor Corporation for its outstanding customer service. Awards are given based on the customer satisfaction ratings received by a dealership. Here's how the dealership uses teamwork to generate customer satisfaction:

1. Someone in marketing sends out letters and postcards to remind customers to bring their cars or vans in for service.

2. When a customer calls to arrange for service, the receptionist in the service department schedules the appointment and verifies the approximate amount of time required for the needed service.

3. The service manager greets the customer when he or she arrives, reviews what is to be done to the car, and again verifies the approximate time needed to complete the work.

4. A mechanic checks the car and performs the initial inspection. She or he contacts the customer if anything unexpected emerges and lets the customer know of any additional costs or time requirements.

5. The mechanic performs the service.

6. The service manager contacts the customer to let the customer know the car is ready.

7. The service manager completes the transaction when the customer arrives, making sure everything is satisfactory.

8. A day later, an employee from the service department contacts the customer to verify that all service was satisfactory and to find out if any problems have surfaced.

9. A week later a customer satisfaction survey arrives in the mail for the customer to complete.

No one person makes great customer service happen in the dealership. It is a true team effort—even though people within the dealership may not see themselves as part of a formal team structure. Everyone within the service department—and, in fact, within the entire dealership—is focused on a common goal of delivering the highest possible standard of customer service and achieving the highest possible customer satisfaction ratings.

Tools for Assessing Competency

This book contains three assessment tools to help team leaders, managers, team members, and employee groups assess their teamwork competencies and identify opportunities for improvement. Ideally, these assessment tools should be used with other information-gathering methods to get a complete picture of skill gaps and improvement opportunities. The other methods include

◆ interviews

◆ surveys

◆ focus groups.

There are advantages to using each method. By combining techniques, you can get the best possible picture of actual versus desired performance. This information will help you select the best training interventions for your needs and create an implementation strategy for improving performance. Table 3–1 explains how these tools work together to help assess teamwork competencies.

A Recommended Assessment Approach

If your interest in teamwork training is motivated by a request from someone in your organization, Table 3–2 (on page 22) gives you a streamlined assessment approach you can use.

Description of Each Assessment Tool

You will find the three assessment tools in chapter 10 of this workbook. They are for your use in identifying the needs and existing competencies of various groups in your organization. Table 3–3 (on page 23) matches tools to targets. Notice that some tools may be used with multiple groups. You can customize

Table 3–1

Needs Assessment Tools

USE THIS TOOL...	TO GATHER THIS INFORMATION...	FROM THIS GROUP
Individual structured interviews	Performance results and goals of teamwork /ways to customize competency models for ◆ demonstrating teamwork (contributors) ◆ fostering teamwork (leaders)	Senior management Team leaders Department heads Exemplars (people who definitely do what you're wanting everyone to be doing)
Surveys	Opinions about ◆ current teamwork practice ◆ effectiveness of leaders in fostering teamwork ◆ things that contribute to teamwork and things that detract from it ◆ awareness of common goal or focus	Representative segments of a population, possibly including ◆ members of permanent work teams ◆ employees within an organization ◆ members of each management group ◆ formal team leaders ◆ people who have served on project teams
Focus groups	Accuracy of competency models Accuracy of survey results Validity of survey results; explanation of survey responses	Representative segments of the target audience. Focus groups generally consist of four to eight people. You may conduct multiple focus groups.
Assessment tools (provided in this workbook)	Rankings from individuals and teams related to proficiency in and importance of using teamwork behaviors	Members of a formal team Management and/or team leaders Members of a group Employees throughout the organization

items within the tools to align with specific needs in your organization. One important item to customize is the language used within the tool. Do you want to refer to "teams," "groups," "departments," "functional areas," or some other site-specific entity? Select the term or terms most appropriate for your organization.

Table 3–2

Steps for Assessing the Need for Teamwork Training

ASSESSMENT STEP	QUESTIONS TO ASK AND ACTIONS TO COMPLETE
1. Meet with the person requesting training (or sponsoring the training) to discover the underlying problem that led to the training request.	◆ How do you define teamwork? ◆ What goal are people expected to achieve by using teamwork? ◆ What problems is the lack of teamwork causing? ◆ What *measurable* results do you expect to gain if people are effective at demonstrating teamwork or fostering teamwork in others? ◆ How will you measure these results? ◆ Besides lack of skill, what factors could be contributing to the lack of teamwork?
2. Share the relevant competency models with the project sponsor/requester.	◆ Do the models reflect what you want people to know and know how to do? ◆ What behaviors would you add, change, or delete? ◆ Do these behaviors link to the performance results that you indicated are important? ◆ What organization-specific examples can you offer that illustrate the importance of each behavior?
3. Convene one or more focus groups to test the models and the information provided by the sponsor.	◆ Does this model reflect the needs of your group? ◆ What's missing from the model? ◆ What should be changed? ◆ What examples best illustrate the importance of each behavior in your area? ◆ How critical is this competency to your success? To your group's or team's success? To the organization's success?

4. Summarize the data and present them to the project sponsor.	◆ Write a report that summarizes the information you've gathered. In the report, describe
	  ◆ the results that effective teamwork should produce
	  ◆ problems caused by lack of teamwork
	  ◆ the required teamwork behaviors (modified competency models)
	  ◆ any discrepancies between the project sponsor's vision of required results and behaviors and the focus groups' vision
	  ◆ nontraining reasons why teamwork may not be fostered or practiced.
	◆ Have your sponsor sign off on the report before going to the next step.

continued

Table 3–2, continued

Steps for Assessing the Need for Teamwork Training

ASSESSMENT STEP	QUESTIONS TO ASK AND ACTIONS TO COMPLETE
5. Assess current performance and compare it to desired performance.	♦ Select the assessment tools from this book that are most appropriate for your needs. Customize to reflect the competency models you end up with. ♦ Administer to the appropriate group(s). ♦ Collate results. (An Excel spreadsheet can help with this!) The following information is useful: ♦ which skills did the majority of respondents (65 percent or more) label as *important* or *very important* to teamwork? ♦ in which skills did at least 30 percent of respondents indicate they could benefit from greater proficiency? ♦ what skills did people view as *unimportant* or *not very important*? ♦ Compare data to the information you have on desired performance. ♦ Based on the data, identify the training workshops and nontraining activities that are likely to be most helpful in building skill and addressing needs.

Table 3–3

Matching Assessment Tools to Target Groups

TARGET GROUP	TOOL(S) TO USE
Department managers, unit managers, team leaders	♦ Is Teamwork Happening Where You Are? (Assessment 10–2) ♦ Organizational Teamwork Assessment (Assessment 10–1)
Members of an intact team	♦ Am I a Team Player? (Assessment 10–3) ♦ Organizational Teamwork Assessment (Assessment 10–1)
Employees within an entire organization	♦ Organizational Teamwork Assessment (Assessment 10–1) ♦ Am I a Team Player? (Assessment 10–3)
Senior management	♦ Organizational Teamwork Assessment (Assessment 10–1)

What to Do Next

- ◆ Make sure you understand the assessment process described in this chapter.

- ◆ Decide what you want to assess and the approach you want to use to do so.

- ◆ Given your goals, conduct an assessment. Use the appropriate tools to gather data.

- ◆ Based on the assessment results, develop an implementation strategy to foster performance improvement. (An implementation strategy template is included in chapter 11.)

- ◆ Select the appropriate workshops to deliver; recommend appropriate nontraining activities for managers to implement (see chapter 7).

◆ ◆ ◆

You've learned what the competencies are, and you've identified ways to assess them within your own organization. Assuming someone has expressed a need for teamwork training, you are ready to move forward by selecting the appropriate interventions. Once you've done so, you should gain executive buy-in to the intervention. The briefing in the next chapter can help you gain this buy-in and make sure efforts to develop teamwork within an organization will be supported.

Gaining Executive Buy-In: A 90-Minute Overview for Senior Managers

What's in This Chapter?

- Questions to help senior management identify the organization's commitment to and support for teamwork

- Lists of training objectives, materials, and preparatory steps for the executive briefing on teamwork

- Sample agenda for the 90-minute overview workshop

Management commonly offers verbal support of teamwork—sometimes going so far as to identify teamwork as a core competency within their organizations. However, *saying* teamwork is a core competency and *creating an organizational climate* that truly supports teamwork are two different things. If your organization says it values teamwork and is asking for training to promote it, senior managers need to ask these questions:

- Are we clear about how we expect teamwork to help us achieve business results?

- How are we communicating this vision throughout the organization?

- What examples can we share to illustrate the power of teamwork and its value to our organization?

- What examples illustrate problems caused by lack of teamwork?

- How does our company incentive program support teamwork? Do we reward teamwork or do we focus rewards on individual accomplishments?

- Do we encourage collaboration and cooperation among individuals and work groups, or do we encourage competition among individuals and groups?

- Can team leaders and/or department managers come to us with problems, or do we view such behavior as a sign that they can't handle their jobs?

- Do we entrust our management and teams with the power to make decisions, or do we discourage decision making at the team or manager level?

This chapter presents a 90-minute executive briefing to help senior managers understand their role in promoting teamwork throughout the organization. It helps senior managers evaluate the existing teamwork climate and prepare to support teamwork throughout the organization. Before you launch into the workshops on fostering teamwork and developing teamwork skills, use this briefing to ensure that senior managers can support the skills and behaviors you plan to help trainees learn.

Training Objectives

The objectives of the executive briefing are to

- describe the benefits of effective teamwork, the factors that contribute to it, and the factors that hinder its development and implementation

- evaluate the level of teamwork currently occurring within the organization

- identify senior management's role in promoting and supporting teamwork throughout the organization

- define the competencies for fostering teamwork and for developing teamwork, and identify the key behaviors taught in the teamwork workshops.

Materials

If any of the learning activities included here require additional supplies, those supplies will be listed with the description of the activity in chapter 8.

For the instructor:

- Projector, screen, and computer for running the PowerPoint presentation

- PowerPoint slides 4–1 through 4–10. (To access the slides for this program, open *Executive Overview.ppt* on the accompanying CD. Copies of the slides for this training course are included at the end of this chapter.)

- A pad of blank flipchart paper, easel, and marking pens

- One folder per participant

- Flipchart pages containing an enlarged version of the organization self-assessment (Assessment 10–1) and the Competency Models

- Tool 10–1: Email Message to Senior Managers

- Learning Activity 8–1: Organizational Teamwork Assessment Results

- Learning Activity 8–2: Creating an Organizational Climate That Supports Teamwork

- Learning Activity 8–3: Reviewing the Teamwork Workshops

For the participants:

- Red and green sticky dots for marking self-assessment flipcharts

- Assessment 10–1: Organizational Teamwork Assessment

- Handout 9–1: Executive Overview Objectives and Agenda

- Handout 9–2: Teamwork Competency Models

- Handout 9–3: Improving the Organizational Climate

Preparation

Before the session:

1. Send an email or memo of invitation to all senior managers who have employees going through the Fostering Teamwork or Developing Teamwork Skills workshops. Use Tool 10–1 as a sample. State the purpose of the session and its importance in supporting implementation of the entire teamwork endeavor. Ideally, the invitation to this workshop should come from a high-level executive. Include the pre-work assignment, Assessment 10–1. Emphasize the need for attendees to complete the assessment prior to the session.

2. Schedule the session.

3. Prepare and organize materials. Create a folder of materials for each participant and put together an instructor's guide for yourself.

4. Gather supplies for the session.

5. Prepare flipcharts for Learning Activity 8–1. You can enlarge Handout 9–2 for this purpose.

6. Order food and beverages as necessary.

7. If a facilities person will set up the training room, communicate your room setup needs to that person.

8. It's important that you review all of the slides as part of your preparation for the workshop. At this time you should plan explanations and examples for concepts presented in the slides.

Just prior to the workshop:

1. Arrive early on the day of the session.

2. If no facilities person is available to set up the room for you, set it up as follows:

   ◆ Arrange tables in a U-shape if you have a small group (10 or fewer). Use pod shapes if you have a larger group.

   ◆ Post the flipcharts showing the enlarged organizational teamwork assessment and the competency models on the walls where participants can easily see and reach them.

3. Set up a flipchart easel and pad. Make sure markers contain ink.

4. Set up and test the LCD projector (or overhead projector, if you are using transparencies instead of slides).

5. Display PowerPoint slide 4–1 to welcome participants.

6. Greet participants individually as they enter the room. Thank them for taking time to attend.

Sample Agenda

The times assigned to the elements of this workshop are approximate and will vary with discussion and instructor emphasis.

8:30 a.m. Welcome (10 minutes)

Welcome participants to the executive overview session. Introduce yourself. If needed, have participants introduce themselves. (It's most likely that senior managers will already know one another.)

8:40 Workshop objectives and agenda (5 minutes)

Distribute Handout 9–1: Executive Overview Objectives and Agenda. Use PowerPoint slides 4–2 and 4–3 to review the objectives for the session.

8:45 Learning Activity 8–1: Organizational Teamwork Assessment Results (30 minutes)

This activity provides an opportunity for senior managers to honestly discuss the status of teamwork throughout the organization as well as the disparities between their views and the views of the employees who report to them.

9:15 Learning Activity 8–2: Creating an Organizational Climate That Supports Teamwork (30 minutes)

In this activity, participants address the negative assessment results gleaned from Learning Activity 8–1, and they develop a plan for addressing these assessment items.

9:45 Learning Activity 8–3: Reviewing the Teamwork Workshops (15 minutes)

Distribute the agendas and objectives for each workshop and provide senior managers with an overview of the learning design and content of each workshop. At this time help managers recognize the importance of their visible support for the skills being taught.

10:00 Conclude the session (5 minutes)

Use slide 4–10 to summarize the activities completed in the executive overview. Thank participants for attending. Remind them that you (and the person designated during Learning Activity 8–2) will be following up with them to verify that action items are completed.

What to Do Next

◆ Based on your assessment results, prepare for and deliver the workshops appropriate for your organization. These could include the workshop for fostering teamwork, demonstrating teamwork, or both.

◆ ◆ ◆

You've inspired your senior leadership and, hopefully, gained their commitment to support the competencies related to teamwork. Your next task is to deliver the appropriate workshops within the organization. Depending on senior leadership's vision, you may deliver the fostering teamwork workshop (chapter 5) or the workshop for team members (chapter 6), you may provide team-building activities that managers can do, or you may present a combination of these.

Slide 4–1

Fostering Teamwork

An Executive Overview

Slide 4–2

Workshop Objectives

- Describe the benefits of effective teamwork, the factors that contribute to it, and the factors that hinder its development and implementation.

- Evaluate the current level of teamwork occurring within the organization.

Slide 4–3

Workshop Objectives

- Define the competencies for fostering teamwork and developing teamwork skills, and identify the key behaviors associated with each of them.

- Identify their role in promoting and supporting teamwork throughout the organization.

Slide 4–4

Questions to Get Us Started…

- What value does teamwork have in organizations?

- Why is teamwork important to THIS organization?

- How does this organization communicate teamwork's importance and value?

Slide 4–5

Organizational Teamwork Assessment

- **Green** dot by every "yes" response
- 1 **red** dot by every "not sure" response
- 2 **red** dots by every "no" response
- **Yellow** dot by every response where your response differs from those of your employees

Slide 4–6

Compile Results

- On the enlarged flipchart:
  - Mark with a **green** dot any item where there is consensus on YES.
  - Mark with a **red** dot any item where there is consensus on NO.
  - Mark with a **yellow** dot any item where there is disagreement.

Slide 4–7

Create a Plan for Improving
the Climate

- Use Handout 9–3 to
  - Identify issues that need to be addressed.
  - Identify actions to take that will improve these issues.
  - Decide who is accountable.
  - Select a target date for implementation.

Slide 4–8

Workshops Overview

- Workshops are based on competency models.
- Each workshop
  - introduces the competencies
  - identifies the value of teamwork
  - requires participants to assess either
    - their own behaviors in fostering teamwork (Fostering Teamwork Workshop
    - their own behaviors in demonstrating teamwork (Developing Teamwork Skills Workshop).

Slide 4–9

Workshops Overview

- Each workshop
  - uses experiential activities and small- or large-group discussion so participants can see the effect of behaviors associated with each competency and can practice applying these behaviors.
  - explores the "tougher" aspects of teamwork:
    - virtual teaming (team members in separate locations)
    - decision making
    - communication
    - goal clarity
    - clarity of roles and responsibilities.
    - trust
  - requires action planning for learning transfer to the workplace.

Slide 4–10

Summary

- Compiled results of organizational teamwork assessment
- Created plan for addressing any areas of concern on the assessment
- Reviewed contents of Fostering Teamwork and Developing Teamwork Skills workshops.
- Identified actions you can take to support learning transfer

◆

Fostering Teamwork: A One-Day Workshop for Team Leaders and Managers

What's in This Chapter?

- A discussion of the behaviors and skills needed by team leaders and managers who want to foster teamwork among their workers

- Lists of training objectives, materials, and preparatory steps for the workshop

- Sample agenda for the workshop on fostering teamwork

Whether they are managing a formal team or an informal work group, team leaders and managers have a huge role in fostering teamwork. They set the tone for the group, and their leadership dictates whether teamwork happens or it doesn't. It's not enough for people in leadership roles to say they want teamwork to happen. Managers and team leaders must recognize and demonstrate specific behaviors that encourage and nurture teamwork among the people who are part of the team or members of the group. When leaders are effective, they clearly describe the task, gain buy-in, clarify roles and responsibilities, cultivate trust, and communicate effectively with team members. Although few team leaders or managers walk into their roles with these skills fully developed, they can learn the skills by combining training with on-the-job experience.

This chapter presents a one-day workshop that helps team leaders or department managers recognize the behaviors that foster teamwork and begin to develop skill in demonstrating the key behaviors outlined in the Fostering Teamwork Competency Model. Chapter 7, which offers activities for use inside and outside of formal team meetings, can give workshop participants ideas on ways to help build and reinforce teamwork skills associated with the Demonstrating Teamwork Competency Model.

Training Objectives

The objectives of the workshop on fostering teamwork are to

- describe the benefits of effective teamwork, the factors that contribute to it, and the factors that hinder its development and implementation

- evaluate the current level of teamwork occurring within the participant's team, work group, or department

- define the *fostering teamwork* competency and identify the key behaviors associated with it

- assess personal skill levels in fostering teamwork and identify the behaviors most in need of development

- improve personal skill in fostering teamwork through use of simulation team experiences

- develop an action plan for transferring skills to the job.

Materials

If any of the learning activities included here require additional supplies, those supplies will be listed with the description of the activity in chapter 8.

For the instructor:

- Projector, screen, and computer for running the PowerPoint presentation

- PowerPoint slides 5–1 through 5–23. (To access the slides for this program, open *Fostering Teamwork.ppt* on the accompanying CD. Copies of the slides for this training course are included at the end of this chapter.)

- A pad of blank flipchart paper, easel, and marking pens

- Flipchart pages containing enlarged versions of Assessment 10–2 and the Fostering Teamwork Competency Model

- Assessment 10–2: Is Teamwork Happening Where You Are?

- Learning Activity 8–4: Is Teamwork Happening Where You Are?

- Learning Activity 8–5: Tower Building, Part 1

- Learning Activity 8–6: Tower Building, Part 2

- Learning Activity 8–7: Trust Builders and Trust Destroyers

- Learning Activity 8–8: Teamwork War Story—A Matter of Trust

- Learning Activity 8–9: Learning Recap #1

- Learning Activity 8–10: Recognizing and Overcoming Communication Challenges

- Learning Activity 8–11: Bridge Building

- Learning Activity 8–12: Decisions and Other Roadblocks

- Learning Activity 8–13: Learning Recap #2

- Training Instrument 10–1: Tower-Building Exercise, Part 1 (to distribute to leaders of teams during first tower-building activity)

- Training Instrument 10–2: Tower-Building Exercise, Part 2 (to distribute to leaders of teams during second tower-building activity)

- Tool 10–3: Program Evaluation and a Sample Instrument

For the participants:

- A binder for each participant

- Yellow, red, and green sticky dots for use in marking self-assessment flipchart

- Assortment of drinking straws, chewing gum, balloons, string, and pipe cleaners for the tower-building exercise

- Newspaper and masking or cellophane tape for the bridge-building exercise

- Handout 9–2: Teamwork Competency Models

- Handout 9–4: Fostering Teamwork Objectives and Agenda

- Handout 9–6: Teamwork War Story—A Matter of Trust

- Handout 9–7: Teamwork War Story—What Really Happened

- Handout 9–8: Learning Recaps

- Handout 9–9: Decisions and Other Roadblocks

> ◆ Handout 9–10: Recognizing and Overcoming Communication Challenges

> ◆ Training Instrument 10–3: Bridge Building for Fostering Teamwork

> ◆ Training Instrument 10–4: Email Communication

Preparation

Before the workshop:

1. Meet with the course sponsor to discuss expectations and desired outcomes for the course. Make sure the objectives of the workshop match the sponsor's expectations. Ideally, conduct an executive overview on teamwork so executive leadership can fully support the implementation (see chapter 4).

2. Prepare an email or memo of invitation to proposed participants. State the purpose of the workshop and its benefits to them in their daily work. Ideally, the invitation should be sent by the course sponsor. Include the pre-work assignment, Assessment 10–2.

3. Schedule the session. Make sure your location is large enough to accommodate the activities that are part of this workshop. Learners need plenty of space to move around and complete activities. For Learning Activity 8–11, participants will need a large amount of empty floor space.

4. Make sure that your program is positioned around an overall effort to develop employees rather than functioning as an isolated training event. Link the program to a larger organizational initiative or work with the course sponsor to position the program.

5. Prepare and organize all training materials—handouts, training instruments, instructions, tools, training program evaluation forms, PowerPoint presentation, and supporting audiovisual material. Create a participant binder for each learner, and place materials within it. Create an instructor's guide for yourself.

6. Obtain supplies for the workshop.

7. Prepare wallcharts for Learning Activity 8–4, using the flipchart paper. You can enlarge Handout 9–2 and Assessment 10–2 for this purpose.

8. Order food and beverages as necessary.

9. If you have a facilities person to help you with setting up the training room, communicate room setup needs to that person.

10. It's important that you review all of the slides as part of your preparation for the workshop. At this time you should plan explanations and examples for concepts presented in the slides.

Just prior to the workshop:

1. Arrive early on the day of training.

2. If you are setting up the training room yourself, follow these steps:

   ◆ Arrange tables so that people can easily sit in groups of three or four.

   ◆ Place tower-building supplies in the center of each table.

   ◆ Allow enough space between tables for participants to complete the bridge-building activity.

   ◆ Place bridge-building supplies in a convenient location.

   ◆ Post the wallcharts where participants can easily see and reach them.

3. Prepare a flipchart page that lists the day's agenda. Post it on the wall.

4. Set up one flipchart easel and pad at the front of the room where it can easily be seen by participants. Make sure markers contain ink.

5. Set up and test the LCD projector (or overhead projector, if you are using transparencies instead of slides).

6. Display PowerPoint slide 5–1 to welcome participants.

7. Greet participants individually as they enter the room. Thank them for taking the time to attend.

Sample Agenda

The times assigned to the elements of this workshop are approximate and will vary with discussion and instructor emphasis.

8:30 a.m. Welcome (10 minutes)

Welcome participants to the Fostering Teamwork workshop. Introduce yourself. Invite participants to introduce themselves by giving their names, describing the team leadership roles they are currently in, and explaining their motivations for attending the workshop.

8:40 Workshop objectives and agenda (5 minutes)

Distribute Handout 9–4: Fostering Teamwork Objectives and Agenda. Use PowerPoint slides 5–2 and 5–3 to review the objectives for the workshop.

Cover housekeeping details (location of restrooms and refreshments, timing of breaks and lunch, and so forth).

8:45 Learning Activity 8–4: Is Teamwork Happening Where You Are? (30 minutes)

This activity familiarizes participants with the fostering teamwork competency and establishes why teamwork is important within the organization. It also enables them to evaluate their strengths and weaknesses in demonstrating this competency. Finally, it sets the tone for the group sharing that should occur throughout the workshop.

9:15 Learning Activity 8–5: Tower Building, Part 1 (35 minutes)

This activity illustrates what can happen when leaders do not behave in a way that fosters teamwork. Participants see firsthand what happens when leaders fail to (1) gain buy-in to the team's goal, (2) involve the team in determining the best way to accomplish the goal, (3) clarify roles and responsibilities, and (4) create an environment that nurtures teamwork. Many participants will find that it reinforces their assessment results.

9:50 Break (10 minutes)

10:00 Learning Activity 8–6: Tower Building, Part 2 (25 minutes)

Participants repeat the tower-building activity with the conscious goals of fostering teamwork and avoiding pitfalls that hindered team leaders in the first rendition of the activity.

10:25   Learning Activity 8–7: Trust Builders and Trust Destroyers (30 minutes)

This activity sets the stage for the war story activity that follows. Participants consider the behaviors that cultivate or destroy trust within a team as well as the behaviors that help create a positive team environment.

10:55   Learning Activity 8–8: Teamwork War Story—A Matter of Trust (25 minutes)

This activity extends the learning that began with the discussion of trust builders and trust destroyers. Participants review the (true) "war story" and write their own ending for it.

When participants are finished writing, share the actual ending with them (Handout 9–7), and discuss the difference between what participants thought should happen and what actually did. Link their ideas related to trust building and trust destroying to the story.

11:20   Learning Activity 8–9: Learning Recap #1 (15 minutes)

This summary gives participants time to identify key learning points that have occurred so far and how they will apply this learning to their workplace situations. Ask volunteers to share ideas. Link their ideas to the self-assessment results posted by the groups.

11:35   Summary of morning's activities (5 minutes)

Use PowerPoint slide 5–13 to summarize activities and learning.

11:40   Lunch break (1 hour)

12:40 p.m.   Learning Activity 8–10: Recognizing and Overcoming Communication Challenges (40 minutes)

This activity is critical because it sets the stage for the final experiential activity of the day, which focuses heavily on the importance of a good communication strategy in supporting a team's efforts. Use this activity to encourage participants to start thinking about all the ways that bad communication hinders teamwork and ways that good communication fosters teamwork.

1:20   Break (5 minutes)

During this brief break, set up the room for the bridge-building simulation exercise.

1:25   Learning Activity 8–11: Bridge Building (1.75 hours, including a break in the middle of the activity)

This activity should be something of a culminating activity for the day. Although the main learning focus is on communication, this activity gives participants an opportunity to apply what they learned in the morning session about establishing clear goals, gaining buy-in from the group, and cultivating trust. In effect, this activity is an opportunity for people to practice as many of the behaviors associated with fostering teamwork as possible.

3:10   Learning Activity 8–12: Decisions and Other Roadblocks (30 minutes)

This short discussion centers on the remaining two behaviors in the Fostering Teamwork Competency Model—removing roadblocks and developing team-based decision-making and problem-solving processes. The point of the discussion is not to build skill, but to build awareness of the behaviors. (Developing problem-solving and decision-making skills requires a separate workshop!)

3:40   Learning Activity 8–13: Learning Recap #2 (15 minutes)

In this activity, you give participants a few minutes to identify the key learning points gained during the second half of the day and to develop action plans for transferring what they've learned to the workplace setting. Summarize the activities that occurred throughout the entire day and explain how these are linked to the Fostering Teamwork Competency Model.

3:55   Conclude the workshop (5 minutes)

Display slide 5–23 and provide a brief summary of the day. Challenge participants to re-administer Assessment 10–2 in four to six weeks. Invite participants to ask any final questions they have. Distribute the training program evaluation form and ask them to complete and return it to you before they leave the room.

Thank them for attending and taking an active part in the training.

What to Do Next

- If appropriate, prepare for and deliver the one-day session, Developing Teamwork Skills, for employees who are part of teams or departments managed by those men and women who participated in the Fostering Teamwork workshop.

- Provide participants with copies of the team-building ideas offered in chapter 7 of this workbook. Explain that these activities all replicate or extend activities that occur in the Developing Teamwork Skills workshop, so they can either teach or reinforce behaviors covered in that workshop when they work with their teams or employees.

- Follow up with participants in four to six weeks. Encourage them to re-administer Assessment 10–2 at that time.

◆ ◆ ◆

In the following chapter, you'll find the workshop designed for team members or individual contributors. Its focus is on the competency of demonstrating teamwork. Ideally, the workshop on fostering teamwork can complement the workshop on demonstrating teamwork skills.

Slide 5–1

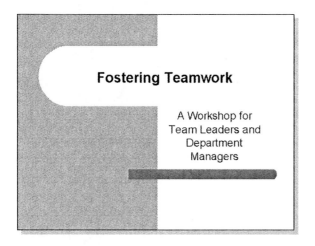

Fostering Teamwork

A Workshop for
Team Leaders and
Department
Managers

Slide 5–2

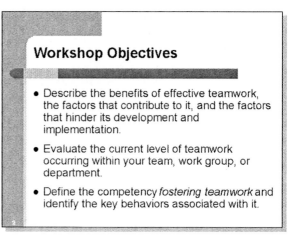

Workshop Objectives

- Describe the benefits of effective teamwork, the factors that contribute to it, and the factors that hinder its development and implementation.
- Evaluate the current level of teamwork occurring within your team, work group, or department.
- Define the competency *fostering teamwork* and identify the key behaviors associated with it.

Slide 5–3

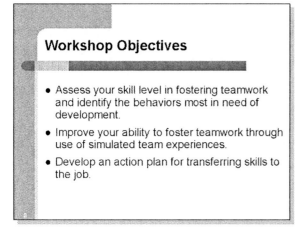

Workshop Objectives

- Assess your skill level in fostering teamwork and identify the behaviors most in need of development.
- Improve your ability to foster teamwork through use of simulated team experiences.
- Develop an action plan for transferring skills to the job.

Slide 5–4

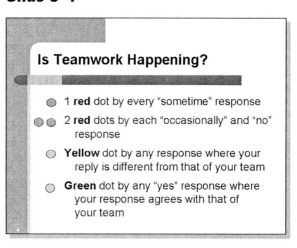

Is Teamwork Happening?

- 1 **red** dot by every "sometime" response
- 2 **red** dots by each "occasionally" and "no" response
- **Yellow** dot by any response where your reply is different from that of your team
- **Green** dot by any "yes" response where your response agrees with that of your team

Slide 5–5

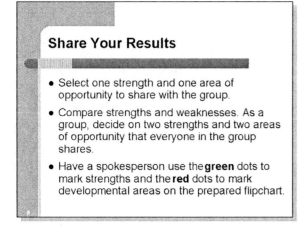

Share Your Results

- Select one strength and one area of opportunity to share with the group.
- Compare strengths and weaknesses. As a group, decide on two strengths and two areas of opportunity that everyone in the group shares.
- Have a spokesperson use the **green** dots to mark strengths and the **red** dots to mark developmental areas on the prepared flipchart.

Slide 5–6

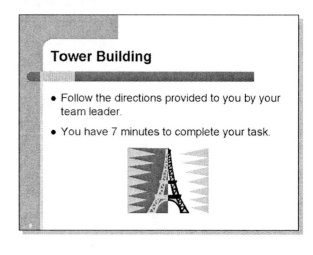

Tower Building

- Follow the directions provided to you by your team leader.
- You have 7 minutes to complete your task.

Slide 5–7

Tower-Building Debriefing, Part 1

- What goal did you clarify with the group?
- Did you let them know the reward would only go to you? What effect does this type of reward structure have on a team?
- Did you solicit ideas on the best way to accomplish the goal? Why or why not?

Slide 5–8

Tower-Building Debriefing

- Did you take time to assign responsibilities or discuss appropriate roles/responsibilities? Why or why not?
- What did you do well? What would you do differently?

Slide 5–9

Tower-Building Debriefing, Part 2

- What goal did your leader communicate?
- What emphasis was placed on the potential team reward?
- How did the leader foster a spirit of cooperation and collaboration?

Slide 5–10

Tower-Building Debriefing

- How were roles and responsibilities defined and clarified?
- Did anyone consider cooperating with another work group? Why or why not?
- How did your team leader respond to the changed criteria for receiving an award?

Slide 5–11

War Story — Recap

- Used the situation as an opportunity to cultivate trust
  - Supported Jane in front of the client; made it clear to the client she still had confidence in Jane's abilities
  - Focused on resolving the problem rather than on assigning blame
  - Modeled teamwork by collaborating with Jane to resolve the problem

Slide 5–12

Learning Recap #1

- Review your behavior self-assessment.
- Think about the activities we've done thus far and how they relate to your self-assessment.
- Identify 1–3 key things you've learned.
- Identify how you can apply this learning in the workplace.
- Use the handout provided to record your ideas.

Slide 5–13

Summary and Morning Wrap-up

- Self-assessment; identification of strengths and areas for development
- Completion of experiential activities (tower building) to illustrate behaviors that hurt or enhance teamwork
- Discussion and war story on trust building/trust destroying and ways to create a positive team environment

Slide 5–14

Effective Communication

- Is timely
- Uses the most appropriate medium available (for example, email, phone, face-to-face meeting, newsletter, and so forth)
- Clearly states the information and identifies the expected response
- Is framed to match the recipient's field of experience (wherever possible)
- Provides a feedback mechanism of some sort

Slide 5–15

What about YOU?

- How do you enhance or hinder the communication within your team or group?
- What example are you setting – positive AND negative?

Slide 5–16

Bridge-Building Simulation

- **Purpose:** To simulate an experience that requires excellent communication for team to be effective in achieving its goal
- **What to do:**
  - Divide into teams.
  - Select a leader and select an observer.
  - Leaders and observers come to the front of the room for instructions.
  - Team members disperse to "geographic locations."

Slide 5–17

Simulation Debriefing

- Order of debriefing:
  - Team leader
  - Team members
  - Observer
  - Facilitator
- Communication issues are discussed first, followed by other key behaviors associated with fostering teamwork

Slide 5–18

Roadblocks

- Anything that hinders a team's ability to get the task completed, such as
  - Lack of resources
  - Conflicts
  - Unrealistic timeline
  - Lack of expertise
  - Inability to make decisions

Slide 5–19

Roadblocks and Decisions

- Follow the directions in Handout 9–9 to answer these questions:
  - What roadblocks did your team encounter that were beyond team members' ability to handle?
  - How did the team leader help remove roadblocks?
  - What decisions did the team have to make?
  - What process did you use for making these decisions?
  - Was your process satisfactory?

Slide 5–20

Accountability Charting

- Clarifies decision making; helps all team members know their roles in the decision-making process
- Provides an objective framework to which the team can refer when confronted with difficult or major decisions
- ***Process note:*** Avoid group accountabilities — they are unwieldy and inefficient.

Slide 5–21

What about Decisions That Are Beyond the Team?

- Not every decision is a team decision — remember the roadblocks beyond the team's scope of responsibility (timeline, resources, $$).
- When a disagreement or problem arises, the first question needs to be, "Is this a problem the team can address?"
- When the answer is "no," the team sets the issue aside and the team leader determines where to go to get a decision.

Slide 5–22

Learning Recap #2

- Review your behavior self-assessment.
- Think about the activities we've done this afternoon and how they relate to your self-assessment.
- Identify 1–3 key things you've learned.
- Identify how you can apply this learning in the workplace.
- Use the handout provided to record your ideas.

Slide 5–23

Workshop Summary

- Assessed current status of teamwork within your departments or teams
- Identified and practiced using key behaviors associated with fostering teamwork
- Identified key learning points throughout the workshop, and developed action plans for implementing learning back in the workplace.
- ***CHALLENGE:*** After four weeks, administer the teamwork assessment to see how you're doing.

Developing Teamwork Skills: A One-Day Workshop for Members of Teams and Groups

What's in This Chapter?

- A discussion of the behaviors and skills needed by team and group members who want to develop teamwork competency

- Lists of training objectives, materials, and preparatory steps for the workshop

- Sample agenda for the workshop on developing teamwork skills

Most employees do not enter the workplace already proficient at working as part of a team or even a group. For many of the reasons outlined in chapter 1, it's common for employees not to know how to work well within a team or group environment. Consequently, if organizations want employees to demonstrate teamwork, they will have to explicitly define what teamwork is and help employees cultivate skill in demonstrating it.

This chapter presents a one-day workshop that helps people who work within teams—or even departments where members sometimes need to collaborate or cooperate. It introduces them to a competency model for demonstrating teamwork and provides skill-building opportunities in the core communication skills associated with teamwork—listening, sharing ideas, acknowledging and resolving disagreements, and providing and receiving feedback.

Training Objectives

The objectives of the workshop on developing teamwork are to

- define the *demonstrating teamwork* competency and identify the key behaviors associated with it

♦ describe the benefits of effective teamwork and the ways team members or group members contribute to or hinder the practice of teamwork

♦ assess one's skill level in demonstrating teamwork, and identify the behaviors most in need of development

♦ improve one's skills in listening, sharing ideas, giving and receiving feedback, and working through conflict during team and group activities

♦ develop an action plan for transferring skills to the job.

Materials

If any of the learning activities included here require additional supplies, those supplies will be listed with the description of the activity in chapter 8.

For the instructor:

♦ Projector, screen, and computer for running the PowerPoint presentation

♦ PowerPoint slides 6–1 through 6–29. (To access the slides for this program, open *Developing Teamwork Skills.ppt* on the accompanying CD. Copies of the slides for this training course are included at the end of this chapter.)

♦ Two blank pads of flipchart paper, easels, and marking pens

♦ Flipchart pages containing enlarged versions of Assessment 10–3 and the Demonstrating Teamwork Competency Model

♦ Five or six rolls of masking tape and a stack of newspapers at least 12 inches high

♦ Assessment 10–3: Am I a Team Player?

♦ Learning Activity 8–7: Trust Builders and Trust Destroyers

♦ Learning Activity 8–9: Learning Recap #1

♦ Learning Activity 8–11: Bridge Building

♦ Learning Activity 8–13: Learning Recap #2

♦ Learning Activity 8–14: What Is Teamwork, and What Is Its Value?

- ◆ Learning Activity 8–15: Effective Communication—The Foundation of Teamwork

- ◆ Learning Activity 8–16: Crossing the Great Divide

- ◆ Tool 10–2: Email Message to Participants in the Developing Teamwork Skills Workshop

- ◆ Tool 10–3: Program Evaluation and a Sample Instrument

For the participants:

- ◆ Red and green sticky dots for marking the self-assessment flipchart

- ◆ A ruler, yardstick, or measuring tape for each team

- ◆ A binder for each participant

- ◆ Handout 9–2: Teamwork Competency Models (first page only)

- ◆ Handout 9–5: Developing Teamwork Skills Workshop Objectives and Agenda

- ◆ Handout 9–8: Learning Recaps

- ◆ Handout 9–11: Effective Communication—The Foundation to Demonstrating Teamwork

- ◆ Training Instrument 10–4: Email Communication

- ◆ Training Instrument 10–5: Bridge Building for Developing Teamwork Skills

- ◆ Training Instrument 10–6: Listening Assessment

Preparation

Before the workshop:

1. Meet with the course sponsor to discuss expectations and desired outcomes for the course. Make sure the objectives of the workshop match the sponsor's expectations. Ideally, conduct an executive overview on teamwork so executive leadership can fully support the implementation (see chapter 4), and a workshop for team leaders or department managers who are responsible for fostering teamwork within a team or group (see chapter 5).

2. Make sure the program is positioned around an overall employee-development effort rather than functioning as an isolated training event. Link the program to a larger organizational initiative or work with the course sponsor to position the program.

3. Prepare an email or memo of invitation to proposed participants. State the purpose of the workshop and its benefits to them in their daily work. Use Tool 10–2 as a sample email. Ideally, the invitation should be sent by the course sponsor. Include the pre-work assignment, Assessment 10–3.

4. Schedule the session. Make sure your location is large enough to accommodate the activities that are part of this workshop. Learners need plenty of space to move around and complete the activities. For Learning Activity 8–11, participants will need a large amount of empty floor space.

5. Prepare and organize all training materials—handouts, training instruments, instructions, tools, training program evaluation forms, PowerPoint presentation, and supporting audiovisual material. Create a binder for each learner and fill it with the participant materials. Create an instructor's guide for yourself.

6. Obtain supplies for the workshop.

7. Prepare flipcharts for Learning Activity 8–14. You can enlarge Handout 9–2 for this purpose.

8. Order food and beverages as necessary.

9. If a facilities person is available to help with setting up the training room, communicate your setup needs to that person.

10. It's important that you review all of the slides as part of your preparation for the workshop. At this time you should plan explanations and examples for concepts presented in the slides.

Just prior to the workshop:

1. Arrive early on the day of training.

2. If no facilities person is available to set up the training room, set it up as follows:

    ◆   Arrange tables so that people can easily sit in groups of three or four.

- Place tower-building supplies in the center of each table.

- Allow enough space between tables for participants to complete the bridge-building activity.

- Place bridge-building supplies in a convenient location.

- Post the flipchart pages on the walls where participants can easily see and reach them.

3. Prepare a flipchart page that lists the day's agenda. Post it on the wall.

4. Set up a flipchart easel and pad. Make sure markers contain ink.

5. Set up and test the LCD projector (or overhead projector, if you are using transparencies instead of slides).

6. Display PowerPoint slide 6–1 to welcome participants.

7. Greet participants individually as they enter the room. Thank them for taking the time to attend.

Sample Agenda

The times assigned to the elements of this workshop are approximate and will vary with discussion and instructor emphasis.

8:30 a.m. Welcome (10 minutes)

Welcome participants to the Developing Teamwork Skills workshop. Introduce yourself. Invite participants to introduce themselves by giving their names, identifying the team roles they are currently in, and explaining their motivations for attending the workshop.

8:40 Workshop objectives and agenda (5 minutes)

Distribute Handout 9–5: Developing Teamwork Skills Workshop Objectives and Agenda. Use PowerPoint slides 6–2 and 6–3 to review the objectives for the workshop.

Cover housekeeping details (location of restrooms and refreshments, timing of breaks and lunch, and so forth).

8:45 Learning Activity 8–14: What Is Teamwork, and What Is Its Value? (30 minutes)

This activity encourages participants to discuss their definitions of teamwork and its value to an organization in general as well as to them personally. It leads into the next activity.

9:15   Learning Activity 8–15: Effective Communication—The Foundation of Teamwork (1.5 hours)

This two-part activity builds listening and communication skills, which are foundational abilities for any team player. Participants complete a listening assessment and then practice basic idea-sharing techniques, which they will use later when they complete a team-based exercise.

10:45   Break (10 minutes)

10:55   Learning Activity 8–7: Trust Builders and Trust Destroyers (30 minutes)

Participants discuss the importance of trust among team members.

This activity sets the stage for the War Story activity that follows. Participants consider the behaviors that cultivate or destroy trust within a team as well as the behaviors that help create a positive team environment.

11:25   Learning Activity 8–9: Learning Recap #1 and a summary of the morning's work (15 minutes)

This summary gives participants time to identify key learning points that have occurred so far and to determine how they will apply this learning to their workplace situations. Afterward, ask volunteers to share their ideas with the group. Link those ideas to the self-assessment results that the groups posted.

11:40   Lunch break (1 hour)

12:40 p.m. Learning Activity 8–16: Crossing the Great Divide (30 minutes)

This activity serves as a warm-up experiential team-building activity. Learners work at listening, sharing ideas, and building trust with each other.

1:10   Learning Activity 8–11: Bridge Building (1.75 hours, including a break in the middle of the activity.)

This activity should be something of a culminating activity for the day. It is designed for both the Fostering Teamwork and the Developing Teamwork Skills workshops. Its main learning focus is on communication and working cooperatively and collaboratively. In effect, this activity represents an opportunity for people to practice as many of the behaviors associated with demonstrating teamwork as possible.

2:55   Conduct Learning Activity 8–13: Learning Recap #2 (15 minutes)

Allow participants a few minutes to identify the key learning points gained during the second half of the day. Ask them to develop action plans for transferring what they learned to their work situations. Then summarize for them the activities that occurred throughout the entire day and explain how these are linked to the Demonstrating Teamwork Competency Model.

3:10   Conclude the workshop (5 minutes)

Display slide 6–29 and provide a brief summary of the workshop. Challenge participants to re-administer Assessment 10–3 in four to six weeks. Invite participants to ask any final questions they have. Thank them for attending and distribute the training program evaluation form. Ask them to complete the evaluation before they leave the training room.

What to Do Next

◆ Follow up with participants in four to six weeks. Encourage them to re-administer Assessment 10–3.

◆ Follow up with participants' team leaders or managers. Find out if and how team skills are being applied.

◆ Encourage participants' team leaders and managers to use the assessment tools as part of team or department meetings. You may also en-

courage them to use one or more of the team-building ideas presented in chapter 7.

◆ ◆ ◆

This chapter, along with chapter 5, provided an excellent foundation for
helping people understand what it takes to foster and develop teamwork
skills. The next chapter provides nontraining activities that managers can use
to reinforce and monitor teamwork competencies.

Slide 6–1

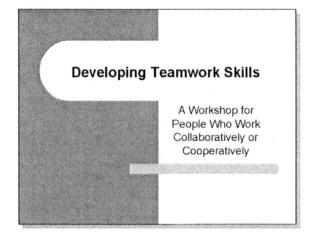

Developing Teamwork Skills

A Workshop for
People Who Work
Collaboratively or
Cooperatively

Slide 6–2

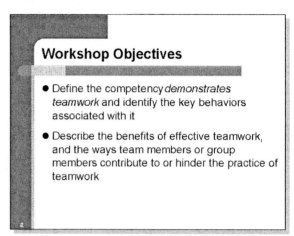

Workshop Objectives

● Define the competency *demonstrates teamwork* and identify the key behaviors associated with it

● Describe the benefits of effective teamwork, and the ways team members or group members contribute to or hinder the practice of teamwork

Slide 6–3

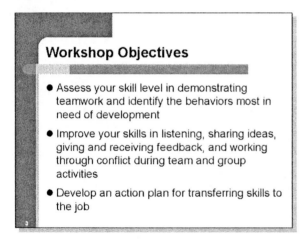

Workshop Objectives

● Assess your skill level in demonstrating teamwork and identify the behaviors most in need of development

● Improve your skills in listening, sharing ideas, giving and receiving feedback, and working through conflict during team and group activities

● Develop an action plan for transferring skills to the job

Slide 6–4

Am I a Team Player?

Slide 6–5

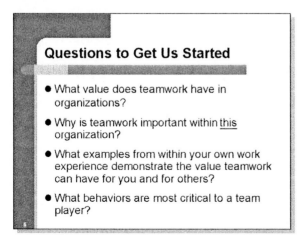

Questions to Get Us Started

● What value does teamwork have in organizations?

● Why is teamwork important within this organization?

● What examples from within your own work experience demonstrate the value teamwork can have for you and for others?

● What behaviors are most critical to a team player?

Slide 6–6

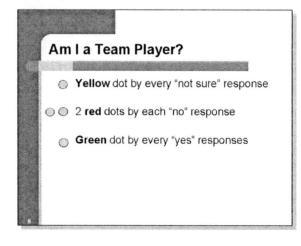

Am I a Team Player?

◯ **Yellow** dot by every "not sure" response

◯ ◯ 2 **red** dots by each "no" response

◯ **Green** dot by every "yes" responses

Slide 6–7

Share Your Results

- Select one strength and one area of opportunity to share with your group.

- Compare strengths and weaknesses. As a group, decide on two strengths and two areas of opportunity that everyone in the group shares.

- Have a spokesperson use the **green** dots to mark strengths and the **red** dots to mark developmental areas on the prepared flipchart.

Slide 6–8

Are You Listening... or Waiting to Talk?

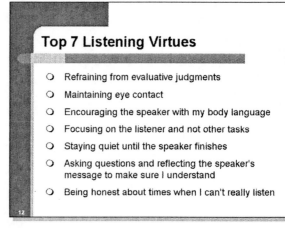

Slide 6–9

The Listening Skills Inventory

- Answer all questions on the listening skills inventory from your own point of view.

- Then, re-take the assessment, responding the way you think a co-worker, team member, or a family member would rate you.

- Calculate both scores. The one associated with your co-worker or family member is probably more accurate.

Slide 6–10

7 Deadly Listening Sins

- Based on the inventory and your personal experience, what are the BIGGEST listening faux pas that people commit?

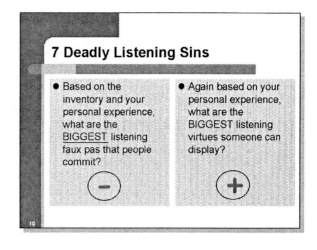

- Again based on your personal experience, what are the BIGGEST listening virtues someone can display?

Slide 6–11

Top 7 Listening Sins

- Making evaluative judgments
- Avoiding eye contact
- Failing to indicate interest via body language
- Multitasking
- Interrupting in the middle of a sentence or story
- Failing to clarify meaning
- Not letting someone know when I can't listen

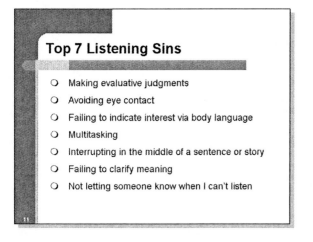

Slide 6–12

Top 7 Listening Virtues

- Refraining from evaluative judgments
- Maintaining eye contact
- Encouraging the speaker with my body language
- Focusing on the listener and not other tasks
- Staying quiet until the speaker finishes
- Asking questions and reflecting the speaker's message to make sure I understand
- Being honest about times when I can't really listen

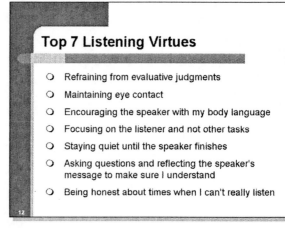

Slide 6–13

Let's Try It

- Select a partner; identify one as the speaker and the other as the listener.

- Speaker talks on a topic of his or her choice for 90 seconds. Listener commits as many of the 7 deadly listening sins as possible.

- Re-do the experience with listener displaying listening virtues.

Slide 6–14

It's not just what you <u>say</u>...

Slide 6–15

Try These...

- It's a nice dress.
- Really, dinner was good.
- You look nice.
- I like your idea.
- Yes.
- No.

Slide 6–16

Consider Nonverbals

- More than 60 percent of the message is <u>nonverbal</u>—facial expressions, body language, tone of voice, and so forth.

- Movement, voice, facial expressions, and gestures affect the impact your message has.

- Most people can dramatically improve their personal effectiveness by focusing on both <u>how</u> and <u>what</u>.

Slide 6–17

Improving Messages

- ❍ Use good word choices and description to create a positive environment and cultivate interest.
  - – When possible, speak in positives rather than negatives.
  - – Stay focused on issues, not people.
  - – Avoid distractors – "you know," "uhmmm," "okay."
  - – Use people's names whenever possible.
  - – Consider the **imagery** that words convey: warm, hot, stifling, suffocating, sweat-inducing, and the like.

Slide 6–18

Let's Try It

- **Positives instead of negatives:**
  - ❍ I **don't** think your idea will work.
  - ❍ We **don't** need another meeting.
  - ❍ We **can't** have this ready by Friday.
- **Word imagery and specificity:**
  - ❍ It's cold out.
  - ❍ You did a nice job.
  - ❍ Your report looks good.
  - ❍ You did a poor job.

Slide 6–19

Improving Messages

m Use your eyes, voice, and gestures to maintain engagement.

- Eye contact pulls listeners in.

- Pacing, tone, and volume affect listeners' engagement

- Meaningful gestures add interest and release energy/anxiety. (I'm not talking about nervous habits!)

Slide 6–20

Let's Try It

- Work in threes, with each person playing the role of speaker for one round of the exercise.

- Speaker is to address the topic "The Most Important Attribute of a Team Player" with the listeners.

- Each speaker gets to talk for 1 minute, and should apply the following:
  - word choices to create a positive environment
  - eyes, voice, and gestures to engage listeners.

- Listeners, apply listening techniques!

Slide 6–21

Quickie Tips on Email

- When in doubt, do not send! Save the message in draft mode instead.

- Avoid lengthy emails; if it's longer than two paragraphs, consider a follow-up phone call.

- Don't attempt to resolve conflicts via email.

- KNOW THAT **BOLDFACE** AND ALL CAPS ARE WAYS OF SHOUTING AT YOUR READER.

- Use the subject line to let the reader know the subject!

- Avoid over-use of Reply button.

Slide 6–22

Quickie Tips on Email

- Consider whether a phone call would be better, faster, or less likely to result in a misunderstanding.

- Remember the limits of email—you lose all the nonverbal signals that can help convey a message. **Tone** still comes through, however, so watch your language.

Slide 6–23

Summary and Morning Wrap-up

- Self-assessment; identification of strengths and areas for development

- Completion of activities related to listening and idea sharing

- Discussion of trust building/trust destroying and ways to help create a positive team environment

Slide 6–24

Tower-Building Debriefing

- What goal did you clarify with the group?

- Did you let them know the reward would only go to you? What affect does this type of reward structure have on a team?

- Did you solicit ideas on the best way to accomplish the goal? Why or why not?

Slide 6–25

Crossing the Great Divide

- Divide into teams of 5–7 people.
- Teams stand along one side of the masking tape "divide" with outsides of feet touching teammates' feet.
- Goal is for team to cross to the other side of the "divide" without breaking foot contact.
- Teams who do break contact must return to the starting line and try again.

Slide 6–26

Bridge-Building Simulation

- **Purpose:** To simulate an experience that requires excellent communication for team to be effective in achieving its goal
- **What to do:**
  - Divide into teams.
  - Select a leader and select an observer.
  - Leaders and observers come to the front of the room for instructions.
  - Team members disperse to "geographic locations."

Slide 6–27

Simulation Debriefing

- Order of debriefing.
  - Team leader
  - Team members
  - Observer
  - Facilitator
- Communication issues are discussed first, followed by other key behaviors associated with demonstrating teamwork.

Slide 6–28

Learning Recap #2

- Review your behavior self-assessment.
- Think about the activities we've done this afternoon and how they relate to your self-assessment.
- Identify 1–3 key things you've learned.
- Identify how you can apply this learning in the workplace.
- Use the handout provided to record your ideas.

Slide 6–29

Workshop Summary

- Assessed current status of your teamwork behaviors
- Identified and practiced using key behaviors associated with demonstrating teamwork
- Identified key learning points throughout the workshop, and developed action plans for implementing learning back in the workplace
- *CHALLENGE:* After 4 weeks, re-take the teamwork assessment to see how you're doing.

◆

Team-Building Activities for Use with Departments and Teams

Training can get employees moving along a path in the right direction. However, maintaining strong teamwork behaviors requires constant monitoring and dialogue. On the following pages, managers and team leaders will find four different activities they can facilitate—either as part of a regular meeting or as a special team-building effort. Most of these exercises either replicate or extend an activity that occurs in the formal teamwork workshops—and so will reinforce the lessons learned in the workshop. The activities can also stand alone—that is, participants do not have to have completed the workshops to benefit from these exercises.

Note: These activities assume a relatively healthy work environment. If there are significant problems within a team or a work environment, then these activities may not be successful. In such cases, an external, objective facilitator would probably be more effective in addressing the team's or group's problems and issues.

Team-Building Activity 1: 360-Degree Feedback

PURPOSE

This activity is designed to enable managers, team leaders, team members, and department employees to honestly share what's working and what's not working with the ways that teams are functioning and the ways that teams are being led.

Note: When doing this activity, managers or team leaders need to guarantee anonymity of responses. Employees may not be forthcoming and honest if they believe negative answers can be traced back to them.

MATERIALS

- ◆ One copy of Assessment 10–2: Is Teamwork Happening Where You Are? and of Assessment 10–3: Am I a Team Player? for each person on your team, including yourself

- ◆ One additional copy of each assessment for yourself on which you can collate the results from the group

TIME

- ◆ Allocate 20 to 60 minutes of meeting time for this activity, depending on team size. A team of two to three members may only require 20 minutes; a team of six or seven members may need an hour.

INSTRUCTIONS

1. Either via email or in person during a staff meeting, give each team member (including yourself) a copy of both assessment tools.

2. Explain that the goal of this assessment activity is for all members of the department or team to get a "pulse reading" of the team's strengths and weaknesses. Note that the team may use the assessment results to develop an action plan for improving its skills in one or more areas.

3. Ask all team or department members to complete both assessments and return them to you within a specific amount of time. If the work is being done via email, ask that assessments are returned within five

workdays. If meeting in person, give everyone 10 minutes to complete the assessments. Be clear in saying that respondents do not have to include their names on the assessments, and that their anonymity will be protected.

4. When the assessments are submitted, collate the results. On your extra copy of each assessment, mark the number of responses made to each item. Be sure to include your own responses in the collated results.

5. Use a highlighter or some other marking tool to identify any items on which significant disagreement exists. Those items are the ones to focus on during a staff or team meeting or discussion.

DEBRIEFING AND FOLLOW-UP

1. Distribute copies of the collated results to all team members or staff members.

2. As a group, select one to three areas for discussion and action planning.

3. For each area selected, have a group discussion and answer the following questions:

    ◆ Why is this an area of opportunity for our team?

    ◆ What are we doing now that makes us less effective than we could be?

    ◆ What should we be doing?

    ◆ What's preventing us from doing it?

    ◆ What can we stop or start to encourage improvement in this area?

4. Document the results of the discussion, identifying all action items and who is responsible for each of them. Select a follow-up date (probably four to six weeks in the future) to meet again and evaluate progress.

5. At the follow-up meeting, invite all of the team members to evaluate whether the team improved in its targeted areas. Encourage team members to describe specific examples that illustrate improvement. Acknowledge employees' efforts.

Note: It is appropriate to host a celebration of the team's efforts—a group lunch in a nearby eatery, pizza brought into the department, a coffee break sponsored by you, or some other acknowledgment of work well done. If budget is an issue, consider showcasing one example of the team's improvement by developing a brief PowerPoint presentation, display, or white paper that describes the team's successes and acknowledges everyone's efforts.

Team-Building Activity 2: Improving Team Listening Skills

PURPOSE

This activity is designed to help develop one of the core communication skills required on a team or in a department—listening to others. This activity also helps you improve your own skills at listening to your employees or members of your team.

MATERIALS

- ♦ One copy of Training Instrument 10–6: Listening Assessment for every person on your team or in your department, including yourself.

- ♦ Whiteboard or flipchart with easel, and marking pen

TIME

- ♦ 20–40 minutes, depending on team size

INSTRUCTIONS

1. During a staff or team meeting, give each team member, including you, a copy of the training instrument.

2. Review the directions on the assessment, and have everyone complete it. Ask them to include their names on the assessment.

3. When everyone has finished the assessment, ask each person to calculate his or her scores, note them for themselves, and pass the assessments to you.

4. On a whiteboard or flipchart, note the scores and identify the score ranges: 14–15, excellent listener; 12–13, good listener; 10–11, needs improvement; 9 or less, needs significant development.

5. Ask members to tell you the items they missed. Document these on the whiteboard or flipchart.

DEBRIEFING AND FOLLOW-UP

1. As a group, strategize ways to improve scores. Identify specific behaviors on which everyone can try to focus.

2. As a group, commit to improving listening skills over the next two weeks. Encourage all employees to give each other feedback on positive and negative listening behaviors observed during those two weeks. Agree to reconvene and retake the assessment at the end of that period. Some improvement in each person's listening skill and assessment score will be the goal.

3. At the end of two weeks, repeat the activity and measure improvement. Be prepared to celebrate successes in some way—perhaps by handing out some type of clever reward (such as a pair of big ears) to all those who improved their scores. (**Note:** Here are two Websites that offer inexpensive novelty items: www.jokeitem.com and www.orientaltrading.com. There are many others on the Web.)

Team-Building Activity 3: Idea Sharing

PURPOSE

This activity is designed to help all team members and employees improve their ability to share ideas with each other and to recognize the effects that nonverbal signals can have on their message. (Ideally, this activity should follow the one on listening skills.)

MATERIALS

- ◆ Projector, screen, and computer for running the PowerPoint presentation

- ◆ PowerPoint presentation *Idea Sharing.ppt*, included on the accompanying CD. Copies of the slides in this presentation (slides 7–1 through 7–7) are included at the end of this chapter.

TIME

- ◆ 30 minutes

INSTRUCTIONS

1. Before you meet with your team or the members of your staff, review the slide contents. The Notes Page view of the file offers tips for what to say in connection with each slide. (To access this view, click on VIEW in the menu bar at the top. Then select NOTES PAGE.)

2. Identify the key points you want to make in association with each of the slides.

3. During a 30-minute meeting, go through the presentation with your employees or team members and complete the activities that are part of it.

DEBRIEFING AND FOLLOW-UP

1. After completing the activities, invite each team or group member to choose one to two idea-sharing behaviors she or he wants to improve.

2. As a group, select one behavior on which all members of the group or team can focus.

3. Over a two-week period, encourage all members to give each other positive or constructive feedback when they see that idea-sharing behavior being used or when they see the behavior *not* being used.

4. Reconvene after two weeks to discuss what improvements have occurred in the ways that people share their ideas with each other. Consider offering some type of small token to acknowledge team members' efforts and to reinforce the concept of sharing ideas. For example, small notepads with a light bulb symbol on them would be a reminder of the concept.

Team-Building Activity 4:
Nurturing Trust and Creating a
Positive Environment

PURPOSE

This activity is designed to elicit team or group members' perceptions about the team climate and the level of trust among members, and to define ways to build trust and create a positive environment within the team or group.

MATERIALS

- ◆ Four flipcharts and easels

- ◆ One blue and one red marker

TIME

- ◆ 30–45 minutes, depending on team size

INSTRUCTIONS

1. Prepare four flipcharts. Label them as follows: *Trust Builders, Trust Destroyers, Environment Builders, Environment Destroyers.*

2. Convene a 30- to 45-minute meeting of the members of your team or group.

3. Ask participants to select a "scribe" and give that person a blue marker.

4. Have everyone spend three minutes in front of each of the four flipcharts. Ask them to brainstorm what you and members of the team *currently* do to build trust, destroy trust, create a positive environment, or hinder development of a positive environment. Instruct the scribe to write the group's ideas on each flipchart.

5. Review the results of everyone's efforts and discuss both the positives and negatives that are happening. Invite people to share examples of both the good and the bad. Urge everyone to stay focused on issues rather than personalities, and encourage them to be honest in their assessments. Be prepared to hear what you may be doing that undermines trust or a positive environment. (If you completed team-building activities 2 and 3 with your employees, remind people to model these skills during this discussion.)

6. Next, give the scribe a red marker. Ask everyone to focus on the flipcharts labeled *Trust Builders* and *Environment Builders*. Invite them to spend three minutes brainstorming ways you or other members of the team or group *could* build trust or the environment—things the group isn't doing now but conceivably might do. Ask the scribe to write each idea on the flipcharts. Encourage participants to identify realistic actions. For example, giving everyone a 10 percent raise is probably not realistic because it's likely not within your or the employees' control.

7. As a group, discuss each idea and let everyone embellish or improve on the ideas they like best.

8. Select one to three ideas to implement.

FOLLOW-UP

1. With the group, schedule a meeting to follow up on implementation within four to six weeks.

2. During the follow-up meeting, discuss how implementation is going. Identify what changes are occurring. Ask participants to describe the team climate and the level of trust they perceive. Make modifications as needed to ensure success.

 ## What to Do Next

◆ If you and your team have not participated in the Fostering Teamwork or Developing Teamwork Skills workshops, consider requesting them.

◆ If training is complete and you would like additional team-building ideas, consult the For Further Reading section at the back of this book for resource ideas.

◆ ◆ ◆

Coming in the next chapter are the learning activities that the teamwork training workshops incorporate. Their descriptions contain lists of instructor and participant materials and detailed instructions for conducting the activities.

Slide 7–1

It's not just
<u>what</u> you say...

Slide 7–2

Try these...

- I have an idea.
- You're not listening to me.
- You want to do what?
- I like your idea.
- Have you considered what it will take to implement your idea?
- Could you get to the point?

Slide 7–3

Consider Nonverbals

- More than 60 percent of the message is <u>nonverbal</u> – facial expressions, body language, tone of voice, and so forth.
- Movement, voice, facial expressions, and gestures affect the impact of your message.
- Most people can dramatically improve their personal effectiveness by focusing on both <u>how</u> and <u>what</u>.

Slide 7–4

Improving Messages

- Use good word choices and description to create a positive environment and cultivate interest.
  - When possible, speak in positives rather than negatives.
  - Stay focused on issues, not people.
  - Avoid distractors – "you know," "uhmmm," "okay."
  - Use people's names whenever possible.
  - Consider the **imagery** that words convey.
    - Nice, good, bad, excellent, mediocre – what image is conveyed by each word? How can you support each word with better imagery?

Slide 7–5

Let's Try It

- **Positives instead of negatives:**
  - I **don't** think your idea will work.
  - We **don't** need another meeting.
  - We **can't** have this ready by Friday.
- **Word imagery and specificity:**
  - My idea will save money.
  - My idea will save time.
  - You did a nice job.
  - Your report looks good.
  - This report does not meet expectations.

Slide 7–6

Improving Messages

- Use your eyes, voice, and gestures to maintain engagement.
  - Eye contact pulls listeners in.
  - Pacing, tone, and volume affect listeners' engagement.
  - <u>Meaningful</u> gestures add interest and release energy/anxiety (I'm not talking about nervous habits!)

Slide 7-7

Let's Try It

- Work in threes with each person playing the role of speaker for one round of the exercise.
- Speaker is to discuss the topic, "The Nonverbal Cues I Look For," with the listeners.
- Each speaker gets to talk for one minute. They are to apply
  - word choices to create positive environment
  - eyes, voice, and gestures to engage
- Listeners, apply listening techniques!

Learning Activities

What's in This Chapter?

- ◆ Tips for facilitating experiential activities

- ◆ Sixteen learning activities for use with the workshop sample agendas

- ◆ Objectives, materials lists, and complete instructions for conducting and debriefing the learning activities

This chapter presents all of the learning activities that are used in the workshops described in chapters 4, 5, and 6. Each learning activity includes the following sections:

- ◆ **Objectives:** A description of what learners will know, will be able to do, or will believe as a result of completing the activity.

- ◆ **Materials:** A list of the supplies, handouts, and training tools and instruments you will need to conduct the activity. A master copy of each handout, training instrument, and tool appears in chapters 9 and 10 and as a .pdf file on the accompanying CD.

- ◆ **Time:** The estimated time required to complete the activity is noted. Exact times, however, do depend on the number of participants in the training. The time estimate includes time required to introduce, conduct, and debrief the activity. You should assume that you will spend at least as much time debriefing the activity as you do conducting it.

- ◆ **Preparation:** This section identifies what you need to do to prepare for the activity. Be sure you study the preparation steps for *all* the activities that are part of the workshop. Some preparations can be completed just before you do the activity; others should be done before the workshop starts. Possible advance work could include arranging the room, preparing flipcharts, posting wallcharts, or acquiring and distributing supplies.

◆ **Instructions:** Each activity includes step-by-step directions for guiding learners through the activity.

◆ **Debriefing:** This section guides you in discussing the key learning points or events that occurred during the activity. I've included extensive comments regarding what types of responses you can anticipate and what key points you need to make. The debriefing is where learning often clicks for people, so don't shortchange it!

Using the Accompanying CD

All the handouts, instruments, assessments, tools, and PowerPoint presentations referred to in the workshops and activities are on the CD that accompanies this workbook. To access these files, insert the CD in your CD drive and click the following file names:

◆ Assessment [number].pdf

◆ Handout [number].pdf

◆ Tool [number].pdf

◆ Training Instrument [number].pdf

The PowerPoint presentations associated with each workshop are identified as .ppt files on the CD.

For information on accessing and printing the electronic files you want to use in your workshops, turn to the appendix at the back of this workbook or read "How to Use This CD.doc" on the CD.

Tips for Facilitating Experiential Activities

These workshops assume an experienced facilitator will deliver them. Key to the success of the workshops is focusing on what learners are to get out of the experiential activities and debriefing these exercises thoroughly. The activities themselves are a means to an end. They provide learners with a common experience upon which they can draw. You may want to let learners know that the activities are designed to help illustrate common pitfalls, common workplace situations, or commonly missing teamwork skills. They are not designed to be clever, difficult, or manipulative.

Show some flexibility as you debrief the activities. I've included extensive debriefing guidelines, but you may identify additional questions or points to make, based on your experience with the group or your organization. Points may emerge during your training session that aren't included in the debriefing guidelines. Be ready to address these situations and the learning that can emerge from them.

You may customize the activities and the tools, handouts, and training instruments. Adjust them to suit the unique characteristics of your organization and your learners. Please remember to observe copyright laws and credit this workbook as your source.

Learning Activity 8–1:
Organizational Teamwork Assessment Results

OBJECTIVES

The objectives of this learning activity are to

- compile the results of the organizational assessment

- identify strengths and areas that need to be addressed for the organization to fully support the practice of teamwork.

MATERIALS

The materials needed for this activity are

- Assessment 10–1: Organizational Teamwork Assessment. (This is pre-work. Participants should be sent this document prior to the workshop with instructions to bring the completed assessment to the session.)

- Yellow, green, and red sticky dots

- PowerPoint slides 4–4, 4–5, and 4–6

- One pad of blank flipchart paper, two easels, and markers

- Wallchart showing the competency model for Demonstrating Teamwork (the first table in Handout 9–2: Teamwork Competency Models)

TIME

- 30 minutes

PREPARATION

- Enlarge the organizational assessment, the Fostering Teamwork Competency Model, and the Demonstrating Teamwork Competency Model into wallcharts. Hang the charts in the training room.

- Make sure all participants are sent Assessment 10–1 as part of their pre-work assignment. In any advance communication with participants, stress the importance of completing this tool before attending the session, and remind them to bring it with them.

INSTRUCTIONS

1. Direct participants to look at Handout 9–2. Explain that it defines the competencies of fostering teamwork and of demonstrating teamwork. It also identifies the key behaviors associated with each competency. The models are based on research done with actual teams and on literature on teamwork (see the sources listed in the For Further Reading section at the back of this workbook). The organizational teamwork assessment that participants completed before the executive session is based on these models.

2. Display slide 4–4. Explain that these models identify behaviors required to foster and demonstrate teamwork. If the employees who work for the organization are truly to value teamwork, they need to buy into its value to themselves and the organization. Ask participants the following questions, and be prepared to share your own examples if participants struggle to get started.

    ◆ **What value does teamwork have in organizations?** (Possible responses: *Getting tasks done faster, getting better-quality ideas or problem solving, bringing together expertise that simply doesn't reside in any one person, accomplishing goals that one person working alone could not accomplish*)

    ◆ **Why is teamwork important within this organization?** (Participants will have a variety of responses, but probe for some specific examples, such as *because it reduces our time to market with a new product, because it gives us a competitive advantage, because it saves us x dollars in manufacturing costs.*)

    ◆ **How does this organization communicate the importance and value of teamwork?** (Encourage participants to be thoughtful in their responses to this question. If communication is limited to statements saying, "We value teamwork," or "We want teamwork," then communication is probably ineffective. Communication involves actions as well as words. How do senior managers *show* they value teamwork? Do they recognize people for it? Do they routinely make time to discuss team endeavors with the employees who report to them? Do they share success stories and lessons learned?

Allow several participants to respond to each question. The goal of these questions is to help participants establish a reason *why* they should care about teamwork and what message the organization is sending to employees about teamwork.

3. Acknowledge participants' efforts at articulating the value of teamwork within the organization (or being honest in pointing out that the organization does *not* sufficiently value it or communicate its value). Explain that the self-assessment managers took prior to the overview session can help senior executives determine how well they are communicating the importance of teamwork and whether the climate is one that fosters teamwork.

4. Display slide 4–5. Direct participants to use their yellow, red, and green sticky dots to mark their assessments according to the directions on slide 4–5. Participants are to use their green dots to mark their **yes** responses and the red sticky dots to mark **no** or **not sure** responses. If participants had their employees complete the assessment tool as well (and that is preferred), participants should use yellow dots to indicate any item for which their response differs from the response(s) of those who report to them.

5. Display slide 4–6.

DEBRIEFING

1. Review the results on the flipchart. Point out the areas of strength (consensus *yes* response) within the group. Invite participants to share examples of what's taking place inside the organization to make these items *yes* responses. You do this to make sure that participants can support their *yes* responses.

2. Shift the focus to the *no* responses. Ask participants to share why these items rate a *no*. Ask them to identify the potential ramifications of the *no* responses. Point out that *no* indicates the organization may have trouble supporting the teamwork competency. These areas need to be addressed by senior executives to ensure the success of any effort to enhance teamwork throughout the organization.

3. Shift focus to the items marked with yellow dots—the items on which there is disagreement. Invite participants to talk about what the yellow dots could signify. Encourage them to consider the possi-

bility that, as a group, senior managers (1) may not have an accurate picture of what's going on within the organization, (2) may not be effectively communicating with their direct reports, or (3) may be sending conflicting messages—verbally supporting the concept of teamwork but maintaining barriers to employees' ability to practice it. Identify these items as opportunities for discussion throughout the organization.

4. Thank participants for compiling results. Tell them that the next activity will help them identify ways in which they can improve the climate to better support teamwork.

Learning Activity 8–2:
Creating an Organizational Climate
That Supports Teamwork

OBJECTIVE

The objective of this learning activity is to identify ways to address the assessment results.

MATERIALS

The materials needed for this activity are

* Handout 9–3: Improving the Organizational Climate

* PowerPoint slide 4–7

* One or two pads of blank flipchart paper (depending on number of teams), easels, and markers

* Enlarged version of the organizational teamwork assessment (used in Learning Activity 8–1)

TIME

* 30 minutes

PREPARATION

* None

INSTRUCTIONS

1. Direct participants' attention to Handout 9–3. Explain that they need to address the *no* areas and the areas of disagreement on the assessment.

2. Display slide 4–7 and review the directions. Allow participants 30 minutes to complete an implementation plan. It may be helpful to assist the group in defining issue statements. For example, participants may want to group two or three items into a single issue statement related to communication or climate. Work with them as needed. If the group is large, identify the issue statements first; then divide issues between two teams and have each group work on half the issues.

DEBRIEFING

1. If participants worked in two separate groups, make sure each group has an opportunity to share its work with the other group. Question the groups to ensure that

    ◆ actions are realistic.

    ◆ actions truly address the issue identified.

    ◆ actions are sufficiently comprehensive (that is, they completely address the problem or issue).

    ◆ accountability is appropriately identified. One common tendency is to assign group accountability too frequently. It's far better to make one person accountable; group accountability tends to provide an escape—no one follows through and no one is accountable for ensuring that others follow through.

    ◆ the timeline is realistic. Participants get very ambitious with timelines—setting dates that cannot be met. When the date isn't met, the action may simply be dropped.

2. Conclude the activity by requesting that one person take responsibility for the entire plan. This person's role (and yours) is to follow up with individuals to make sure they, in turn, follow up with their specific action items.

    Note: Your role in keeping this plan in front of senior executives is important. Be prepared to follow up in the weeks after this session to ask them, "How is the action plan going?" and "Have you accomplished your tasks?"

3. Remind participants that teamwork will not happen in the organization if the climate does not support it. The most important role senior managers have in teamwork is creating a climate that is conducive to its development. Senior managers must make their commitment to teamwork audible and visible—speak to the value and importance of teamwork and then demonstrate a belief in their own words.

Learning Activity 8-3:
Reviewing the Teamwork Workshops

OBJECTIVES

The objectives of this learning activity are to

- define the competencies for fostering teamwork and demonstrating teamwork

- identify the key behaviors taught in the teamwork workshops.

MATERIALS

The materials needed for this activity are

- Handout 9–2: Teamwork Competency Models

- Handout 9–4: Fostering Teamwork Workshop Objectives and Agenda

- Handout 9–5: Developing Teamwork Skills Workshop Objectives and Agenda

- Enlarged wallcharts of the Fostering Teamwork and Demonstrating Teamwork Competency Models

- PowerPoint slides 4–8 and 4–9

TIME

- 15 minutes

PREPARATION

- None

INSTRUCTIONS

1. Direct participants' attention to Handouts 9–2, 9–4, and 9–5. Explain that Handout 9–2 contains the competency models upon which each workshop is based. Handouts 9–4 and 9–5 contain the objectives and agenda for each workshop.

2. Display slides 4–8 and 4–9, and briefly describe the design and content of the workshops. Encourage participants to review Handouts

9–4 and 9–5 to see the objectives and agenda associated with each workshop.

3. Invite participants to ask questions about the workshops. Be prepared for them to ask about the experiential activities. You may want to pass out copies of the handouts associated with the tower-building and bridge-building activities for each workshop. Emphasize that the most significant aspect of every experiential activity is the debriefing of the experience. Explain that the activity is the opportunity to illustrate what participants need to learn and discuss.

4. When all questions have been answered, ask participants, "Why is it so important for you to follow through on the plan you created for improving the teamwork climate in the organization?" Your goal is to get participants to recognize that the behaviors promoted in the workshops will not be adopted in the workplace if the organizational climate doesn't support and promote teamwork.

5. Ask participants, "What else can you as a senior manager do to support learning transfer from these workshops?" Get participants to recognize the importance of promoting the workshops themselves and of being familiar enough with their contents to discuss the workshops with employees. You may also want to encourage executives to attend a workshop as a participant. That will send a strong message to all employees about the value that senior managers see in the workshops.

Learning Activity 8–4:
Is Teamwork Happening Where You Are?

OBJECTIVES

The objectives of this learning activity are to

- ◆ define the meaning of teamwork and its value to the organization and to participants within a team

- ◆ enable participants to identify whether and how well teamwork is happening in their work areas.

MATERIALS

The materials needed for this activity are

- ◆ Assessment 10–21: Is Teamwork Happening Where You Are? (This is pre-work. Participants should be sent this document prior to the workshop with instructions to bring the completed assessment to the session.)

- ◆ Yellow and red sticky dots

- ◆ PowerPoint slides 5–4 and 5–5

- ◆ Flipchart paper and markers

- ◆ Wallchart showing the Competency Model for Demonstrating Teamwork (the first table in Handout 9–2: Teamwork Competency Models)

TIME

- ◆ 20 minutes

PREPARATION

- ◆ Make sure that each participant is sent Assessment 10–2 as part of their pre-work assignment. Stress the importance of completing this assessment prior to attending the workshop and bringing it to the session.

- ◆ This activity is the opening activity in the Fostering Teamwork workshop. It is helpful to enlarge the Competency Model for Demonstrating Teamwork (part of Handout 9–2). Hang the enlarged version on the wall of the training room so that everyone can see it.

INSTRUCTIONS

1. Direct participants' attention to Handout 9–2. Explain that it defines the competency of demonstrating teamwork and identifies the key behaviors associated with it. This model is one that has been validated by numerous managers and team leaders. The team behavior inventory participants completed prior to the training is based on this competency model.

2. Explain that the second model within Handout 9–2 identifies behaviors that *foster* teamwork. However, participants need to buy into the value of teamwork before the model for fostering teamwork can have real meaning. Ask participants the following questions, and be prepared to share your own examples if participants struggle to get started.

    ◆ **What value does teamwork have in organizations?** (Possible responses: *Getting tasks done faster, getting better-quality ideas or problem solving, bringing together expertise that simply doesn't reside in any one person, accomplishing goals that one person working alone could not accomplish*)

    ◆ **What examples can you think of that demonstrate the value of teamwork to an organization?** (Generic examples may include *discovery of an invention, a product launch, manufacture of a product, sales teams.*)

    ◆ **What examples from your own work experience demonstrate the value of teamwork?**

    ◆ **What happens when teamwork is absent?**

    ◆ **From your work or personal life can you describe one example of working on a team and having a leader who enabled the team to function extremely well? What did the team leader do to help make this happen?** (Typical examples include *sports teams* and *political or community project committees.*)

    ◆ **Can you give an example of being on a team that didn't function well? How did the team leader contribute to the team's problems?**

    Allow several participants to respond to each question. The goal of these questions is to help them establish a reason *why* they should care about fostering teamwork, and to help them begin to think about what behaviors nurture it and what behaviors prevent it from happening.

3. Display slide 5–4. Note that participants have done an excellent job helping point out reasons why teamwork is important. The self-assessment will help establish how they can improve their own skills in fostering teamwork. Explain that participants are to use their red and yellow sticky dots to mark their team behavior inventories. Participants are to use their red dots to mark behaviors that received anything other than a *yes* response. Any item that received an *occasionally* or a *no* response gets a second red dot. The yellow sticky dots are used to mark any items on which the team members' response differs from the manager's or leader's response.

4. Display slide 5–5. Explain that participants are to discuss the assessment results. After individually marking their strengths and areas of opportunity, each person should decide which one strength and which one area of opportunity he or she wants to share with the group. Explain that the goal is for participants to identify what they have in common and what they can learn from each other.

5. Tell participants that, as a group, they should agree on the top two strengths and top two areas of opportunity that they have in common.

6. Instruct group members to use their dots to mark these common areas on the wallchart.

DEBRIEFING

1. Review the results on the wallchart. Point out the areas of strength within the group as well as the areas of opportunity. Ask participants to share what they learned about each other. Invite them to form some conclusions about the consequences of *not* demonstrating the behaviors associated with the competency. *Allow several minutes for this discussion—it's the reason participants are attending this workshop.* Point out that participants can learn from each other—one person can share her successes with someone who is struggling in an area. In areas where the majority of participants have an opportunity for improvement, everyone can learn together.

2. Explain that the goal of the workshop is to help people recognize their strengths and participate in learning experiences that enable them to recognize the value and importance of all the behaviors associated with fostering teamwork. The workshop offers many opportunities for participants to share their own experiences and build skill in practicing the behaviors associated with encouraging and nurturing teamwork.

Learning Activity 8–5:
Tower Building, Part 1

OBJECTIVES

The objectives of this learning activity are to

- ◆ recognize the importance of gaining a team's buy-in to the goal

- ◆ demonstrate the difficulty of achieving the goal when the team does not contribute to planning how to achieve it

- ◆ demonstrate the ineffectiveness of a team for which roles, responsibilities, and accountabilities are not defined.

MATERIALS

The materials needed for this activity are

- ◆ Tower-building supplies: drinking straws, balloons, sticks of chewing gum, string, and a candy bar

- ◆ A measuring tool—ruler, yardstick, or measuring tape

- ◆ Reward for the team leader whose team builds the tallest tower—a candy bar, small toy, novelty item

- ◆ PowerPoint slides 5–6 through 5–8

- ◆ Two flipcharts, easels, and markers

- ◆ Training Instrument 10–1, Tower-Building Exercise, Part 1 (for team leaders only)

TIME

- ◆ 35 minutes

PREPARATION

- ◆ Make sure each table has a supply of drinking straws, balloons, chewing gum, and string.

INSTRUCTIONS

1. Divide participants into groups of three or four, and assign each group a number (Team 1, Team 2, and so forth).

2. Randomly select one person from each group to serve as a team leader. Give each leader a copy of Training Instrument 10–1: Tower-Building Exercise, Part 1. Ask them to review the directions provided there and conduct the exercise. Remember, it is up to the leaders to decide what and how to communicate information to their teams. Don't give them any instructions on that.

3. Display PowerPoint slide 5–6 as the exercise unfolds.

4. Wander among the groups and silently make observations about what teams are doing well and what they are not doing well. Don't offer any commentary to teams during the exercise.

5. Time the teams as they complete the activity.

DEBRIEFING

1. Call time after seven minutes.

2. Write team numbers on a flipchart with space next to each number for recording the tower height.

3. Measure the height of each team's tower. Write the results on the flipchart. Award a prize to the leader of the team whose tower is tallest.

4. Use PowerPoint slides 5–7 and 5–8 to guide the debriefing discussion. Allow ample time to discuss each question and prompt group members to identify the key points associated with each question. The questions and main points that should emerge are these:

   ◆ **What goal did you clarify with the group?** The goal was to build the tallest tower, making it freestanding and strong enough to support a candy bar. However, *the reward was given only for making the tallest tower.* It's common for teams *and* team leaders to do only what they are rewarded for doing. So, clarifying the goal is important. Perhaps the real goal simply is to build the tallest tower. At a minimum, it is important for everyone on the team to understand why making the tower freestanding and strong enough to support a candy bar is important even though it has no bearing on potential rewards. Help the group identify what happens in their work world when people lack clarity on the goal. Encourage learners to talk about times when they either led or participated in an effort for which the goal was poorly communicated or understood. Get them to describe the common effects of such a situation on the team's efforts.

◆ **Did you let them know the reward would only go to you? What impact does this type of reward structure have on a team?** Most people will *not* let the team know that an individual reward is possible. Point out that a team's morale and motivation can suffer when group members discover that rewards go to some people and not others. A team's trust in its leader also suffers when a hidden agenda emerges. Invite the winning team's members to talk about what it feels like to see the leader rewarded. Invite the team leaders to comment on their incentive for involving the group in an effort that was going to reward only the leader. Point out that such structures sabotage the very notion of teamwork. A group needs to see a shared benefit to accomplishing the goal for the goal to matter to the group. The candy bar placed at the top of the tower can represent intrinsic or extrinsic rewards. Money or job promotion is definitely a motivator for people, but so are recognition and acknowledgment of accomplishment.

◆ **Did you solicit ideas on the best way to accomplish the goal? Why or why not?** Time pressure frequently shuts down communication and idea sharing. People get into a mode of "I can do it faster myself." They can also get very directive. A directive tone coupled with the reward structure that focuses on individual achievement set up an environment that does not promote or take advantage of teamwork.

◆ **Did you take time to assign responsibilities or discuss appropriate roles/responsibilities? Why or why not?** Time pressure can tempt people to forego this step. It can seem like a waste of precious time if the project is small and time is short. But teams can't achieve maximum effectiveness if people lack clarity on roles, responsibilities, and accountabilities. Teams also fail to use people in the most effective way when they don't stop to think about who is best suited for specific tasks. Invite participants to talk about times when they saw lack of clarity hinder a group's efforts and times when clarity accelerated a group's efforts.

◆ **What did you do well? What would you do differently?**
Encourage team leaders to review the Competency Model for
Fostering Teamwork (Handout 9–2). Ask them to review the key
behaviors and point out one or two things they did well and one
or two things they would do differently. Use the flipcharts to
make lists of the positives and the negatives. Then invite team
members to make their own observations about what they saw
their leaders do well or ineffectively. Discuss reasons that may
have contributed to a failure to demonstrate desired behaviors
and how to overcome these issues.

Learning Activity 8–6:
Tower Building, Part 2

OBJECTIVE

The objective of this learning activity is to consciously avoid the pitfalls encountered in Part 1 of the tower-building exercise and thereby foster teamwork.

MATERIALS

The materials needed for this activity are

- Tower-building supplies: drinking straws, balloons, sticks of chewing gum, string, and a candy bar

- A measuring tool—ruler, yardstick, or measuring tape

- A reward for all members of the winning team—candy, a small toy, or novelty item

- A flipchart, easel, and marker

- PowerPoint slides 5–9 and 5–10

- Training Instrument 10–2: Tower-Building Exercise, Part 2 (for team leaders only)

TIME

- 25 minutes

PREPARATION

- Make sure each table has a supply of drinking straws, balloons, chewing gum, and string.

INSTRUCTIONS

1. Explain that participants have the opportunity to repeat the tower-building exercise, this time working to avoid pitfalls that occurred the first time.

2. Keep participants in their same groups, but assign a different person the role of team leader.

3. Give a copy of Training Instrument 10–2: Tower-Building Exercise, Part 2, to each team leader. Tell them to review the directions on the instrument and to conduct the exercise.

4. Wander among the groups and silently make observations about what teams are doing well and what they are not doing well.

5. After approximately four minutes, call team leaders over and explain that the winning tower must be the tallest, be freestanding, and must support the weight of the candy bar.

6. Continue your observations of the effort. Make a mental note of any observations you want to offer during the debriefing about how team leaders handle the goal change.

7. Time the teams as they complete the activity.

DEBRIEFING

1. Call time after seven minutes.

2. Write team numbers on a flipchart with space next to each number for recording the height of the team's tower.

3. Measure each tower. Note whether each tower is freestanding. Place a candy bar on the top of each tower to determine its ability to bear the weight. Write results on the flipchart paper. Award a prize to the members of the team whose tower does the best job of meeting all criteria.

4. Use PowerPoint slides 5–9 and 5–10 to guide the debriefing. Allow ample time to discuss each question and encourage group members to identify the key points associated with each question. The questions and main points that should emerge are these:

   ♦ **What goal did your leader communicate?** Once again, the goal was to build the tallest tower, making it freestanding and strong enough to support a candy bar. However, at the beginning of the activity, *the reward was still only based on creating the tallest tower.* Find out how team leaders decided what goal to communicate and work to achieve. Then invite teams to share what happened when the goal changed midway through completion of the effort. Question the group to find out how well leaders gained buy-in and agreement on the goals and then reinforced the mission as it evolved.

♦ **What emphasis was placed on the potential team reward?** Encourage teams to talk about how (and if) the prospect of a reward for the entire team made a difference in the team's motivation and the overall atmosphere of teamwork. Invite participants to transfer the experience to the workplace—how much difference does it make when leaders and organizations emphasize shared rewards and incentives versus individual ones? What happens when no structure is in place to reinforce collaboration? (People will revert to behaviors that gain them individual rewards.)

♦ **How did the leader foster a spirit of cooperation and collaboration?** Answers to this will vary. It's important that you wander the room and make your own observations to the group in the debriefing. Look for behaviors such as involving everyone in planning, making sure that all members have some responsibility for execution of the design, verbal recognition of people's accomplishments and contributions, and efforts to encourage team members to solicit ideas from other teams or members.

♦ **How were roles and responsibilities defined and clarified?** Answers to this question will also vary. During your observations of the activity, look for team leaders who invite people to take responsibility for specific activities—planning, construction, testing, and so forth.

♦ **Did anyone consider cooperating with another work group? Why or why not?** Because a competitive atmosphere was set up (one team wins; all others lose), it's not likely that team leaders even considered the possibility of cooperating with other teams. Cooperation could have taken the form of sharing ideas or sharing supplies. Invite participants to share ideas on how to foster cooperation in their work world—and how to avoid viewing things competitively in the work environment. Ask how cooperation between work areas has helped encourage teamwork in people's departments and teams, and how it may have been an essential part of getting a task done.

♦ **How did your team leader respond to the changed criteria for receiving an award?** A variety of answers are possible. Look for examples of leaders involving the entire group in solving the problem of the changes required in the design. Invite people to share stories of how goals frequently can change in the work world, and the importance of leaders clarifying and reinforcing the goal on an ongoing basis.

Learning Activity 8-7:
Trust Builders and Trust Destroyers

OBJECTIVES

The objectives of this learning activity are to

- describe the effect that environment has on a team's performance

- identify behaviors that build or hinder trust

- identify techniques for creating a positive team climate.

MATERIALS

The materials needed for this activity are

- Blank flipchart pages to distribute to teams, and one or two markers for each team

- Tape or pushpins to mount flipchart pages to wall space

- Wallchart with enlarged version of Fostering Teamwork or Demonstrating Teamwork Competency Model (Handout 9–2), depending on the workshop you are conducting

TIME

- 30 minutes

PREPARATION

- Write words *Trust* and *Environment* on a flipchart with space next to each for filling in a definition.

- Mount the competency model wallchart on a wall where all participants can see it easily.

INSTRUCTIONS

1. Ask participants to define the words *trust* and *environment*. Expect a variety of responses, but encourage participants to identify the following:

    - **trust**—belief and confidence that others will do what they say, say what they mean, and represent themselves honestly at all times.

◆ **environment**—the atmosphere or climate that surrounds people in their work. Factors that help shape environment include the physical surroundings, (furniture, building, space), the resources included in it (computers, equipment, supplies), the behavior of the people within it, and the rules that govern it (incentives, communication flow and parameters, work allocation).

2. Divide participants into four groups.

3. Give each group one flipchart page and a marker.

4. Have each group post its flipchart page on a wall of the training room. Instruct them to label their flipchart pages as follows:

   ◆ Group 1: Trust Builders

   ◆ Group 2: Trust Destroyers

   ◆ Group 3: Environment Builders

   ◆ Group 4: Environment Destroyers.

5. Instruct each group to select a scribe who will write ideas on the flipchart page. Explain that groups are to spend three minutes brainstorming behaviors and activities related to their topic. (**Note:** For the Fostering Teamwork workshop, the focus should be on *how a team leader* builds or destroys trust and environment. For the Developing Teamwork Skills workshop, the focus should be on *how a team member* helps build trust and create a positive environment or vice versa.)

6. Tell participants to begin. Time the activity, and call time at three minutes.

7. Instruct groups to move to the set of flipchart pages directly to their left. Give teams two minutes to add their ideas to the lists that have already been started.

8. Call time after two minutes and have teams move again to their left. Repeat the cycle until teams have visited all the flipchart pages and have returned to their original ones.

9. At their original pages, give teams one or two minutes to review the lists there. Then ask them to return to their seats.

10. Review all the lists as a group and invite discussion on specific items. Encourage participants to do the following:

◆ Describe specific examples of how a particular behavior built trust, hindered trust, helped create a positive team environment, or destroyed an environment.

◆ Link trust-builder behaviors to the behaviors associated with creating a positive climate. Encourage participants to recognize the relationship between these behaviors.

11. Review the Competency Model for Fostering Teamwork or for Demonstrating Teamwork, depending on which workshop you are delivering. (In either case, the competency model should be located on the wall). Point out the key behaviors mentioned by participants that correlate to creating a positive environment and cultivating trust.

Learning Activity 8-8: Teamwork War Story—A Matter of Trust

OBJECTIVES

The objectives of this learning activity are to

- identify leadership behaviors that cultivate trust and behaviors that hinder trust

- recognize the importance of trust in fostering teamwork.

MATERIALS

The materials needed for this activity are

- Handouts 9–6: Teamwork War Story—A Matter of Trust, and 9–7: Teamwork War Story—What Really Happened, one copy of each for every participant

- PowerPoint slide 5–11

TIME

- 30 minutes

PREPARATION

- None

INSTRUCTIONS

1. Distribute Handout 9–6: Teamwork War Story—A Matter of Trust.

2. Divide learners into groups of three or four.

3. Tell participants they will have seven minutes to read the story silently and then decide in their groups what Susan's actions should be.

4. Have them begin reading. Call time after seven minutes.

5. Invite each group to discuss how they ended the story. Ask each group to explain how its solution promoted teamwork. Ask the following questions:

   - How would your solution build a climate of trust between Susan and Jane?

- ◆ How would your solution recognize Jane's efforts while also coaching her on ways to improve?

- ◆ Will you share your thoughts on why creating a climate of trust is so important to fostering teamwork?

Look for these ideas to emerge: Trust is a foundational element for fostering teamwork. Without trust, most people hold back on contributing. They hesitate to take risks, and they focus on staying safe rather than on performing to their maximum potential. Without it, it's difficult to be successful at any of the other behaviors that foster teamwork.

6. Now shift focus from what Susan did well to what Susan could have done differently. Ask participants to identify what Susan did that hindered teamwork. Try to find out if anyone recognizes that failing to clarify the goal was the partial cause of the problem. The statement of work clearly specified the client's expectations. However, Susan allowed Jane to convince her that the client was supportive of a less rigorous solution than the one described in the statement of work. Jane and Susan should have reviewed this document carefully and revisited it with the client when they appeared to accept Jane's verbal description of a less rigorous solution. Goal clarification would have eliminated the mismatch between what the client actually received and the client's expectations.

7. Distribute Handout 9–7 to participants so they can see the actual ending to the story.

8. Use PowerPoint slide 5–11 to summarize the ways in which Susan fostered teamwork.

9. If time allows, you may want to invite participants to share one or two workplace examples of how trust helped foster teamwork in their organizations—or how a lack of trust hindered it. They can also speak to the issues of goal clarification helping a team and goal confusion hurting a team's efforts.

Learning Activity 8–9:
Learning Recap #1

OBJECTIVES

The objectives of this learning activity are to

- identify key learning points throughout the course

- create an action plan for implementing on the job what is learned in the workshop.

MATERIALS

The materials needed for this activity are

- Handout 9–8: Learning Recaps

- PowerPoint slide 5–12 (Fostering Teamwork workshop) or slide 6–23 (Developing Teamwork Skills workshop)

- Enlarged self-assessment with participants' red and green sticky dots on it (either Assessment 10–2: Is Teamwork Happening Where You Are, for the Fostering Teamwork workshop or Assessment 10–3: Are You a Team Player? for the Developing Teamwork Skills workshop).

TIME

- 15 minutes

PREPARATION

- None

INSTRUCTIONS

1. Direct participants' attention to Handout 9–8.

2. Display either slide 5–12 (Fostering Teamwork) or slide 6–23 (Developing Teamwork Skills). Review the slide contents. Explain that this is the first of two opportunities for participants to spend a few moments reflecting on learning they have experienced and thinking about how to apply this learning to their job situations. Encourage them to reflect on how their experiences and discussion from the morning's activities will make them better at fostering teamwork

(Fostering Teamwork workshop) or demonstrating teamwork (Developing Teamwork Skills workshop). They should then use the Learning Recap handout to record their ideas.

3. Give participants five to seven minutes to complete the activity (unless all participants finish earlier).

4. Invite individuals to share a key learning point and a way in which they will apply it to their roles in the workplace. Allow several people to share their thoughts.

5. If appropriate (that is, if participants mention ideas that came up during the self-assessment activity), link the learning points to the items that emerged as "areas of opportunity" on their self-assessments.

6. Conclude the activity by thanking participants for sharing and expressing positive comments about the ideas shared. For example, "Thanks to everyone for contributing such worthwhile ideas. It sounds as though the morning's activities have helped you think of several ways you can improve your efforts at cultivating trust, clarifying goals, and so forth." Use whatever wording reflects the actual discussion from your training group.

Learning Activity 8–10: Recognizing and Overcoming Communication Challenges

OBJECTIVES

The objectives of this learning activity are to

- define "effective" communication

- describe the impact that good and poor communication have on members of a team and the overall team environment

- identify communication behaviors and tools that enhance and that hinder effective communication.

MATERIALS

The materials needed for this activity are

- PowerPoint slides 5–14 and 5–15

- Handout 9–10: Recognizing and Overcoming Communication Challenges

- Handout 9–11: Effective Communication—The Foundation to Demonstrating Teamwork

- Pads of 4x6-inch sticky notes, markers for all participants

- Blank flipchart pages and two or three markers per small group

- Tape or pushpins to mount flipchart pages to wall space

TIME

- 40 minutes

PREPARATION

- Write the phrase *Effective Communication* on a blank flipchart.

INSTRUCTIONS

1. Direct participants' attention to Handout 9–10: Recognizing and Overcoming Communication Challenges. Instruct them to use this handout as a notetaking guide throughout this activity.

2. Poll the group to find out how many of them encounter the following situations in their groups or teams (ask for a show of hands on each item):

   ♦ Messages don't reach all members of a team or department.

   ♦ The message changes as it passes from one team member to another.

   ♦ It takes too long to communicate messages throughout a team.

   ♦ Misunderstandings related to interpretation of a message cause conflict.

   ♦ Information is withheld from members of a team, which causes conflict or decreases the efficiency and productivity of one or more members of the team.

   ♦ One person assumes that another will pass along information to other members of a group, but it doesn't happen.

   ♦ An email message generates confusion, anger, or misunderstanding.

   Unless your training group is highly atypical, you will see lots of participants raising their hands. Most people will raise their hand to each item you name.

3. Explain that poor communication is the third major reason why teams struggle or fail. The first two reasons are (1) lack of trust and (2) failure to commit to a common goal, which the group discussed this morning. Note that your focus this afternoon is to help participants define effective communication, recognize common communication pitfalls, and ultimately develop skill in defining and executing an effective communication strategy.

4. Instruct each participant to take a sticky note and write on it a definition of *effective communication*. Tell them to place their notes on the flipchart labeled *Effective Communication*. Give them one to two minutes to write and post their definitions.

5. Quickly scan the notes and group them according to commonalities. For example, some participants may create definitions that offer examples of effective communication; others may focus on what makes communication ineffective. Still others may focus on a more dictionary-style definition.

6. Briefly review all the definitions. Point out where definitions overlap and where people have elaborated or expanded on more basic definitions. Expect a variety of responses and acknowledge the value of everyone's ideas.

7. Display slide 5–14 and point out where participants' ideas matched the main points listed on the slide. Address each item on the slide. Invite participants to offer an example to illustrate the importance of each item. Here are some ideas:

   ◆ **Timeliness:** A message delivered either too early or too late causes problems. If people hear something via the rumor mill before they hear the "official" word, the message has been delivered too late and it competes with multiple variations of itself. If people can't act on the information either immediately or in the near future, then it's delivered too early. (Invite participants to offer examples to illustrate this point.)

   ◆ **Communication media:** Email is probably the most misused form of communication today—both in professional and personal worlds. We send emails when we should pick up the phone or schedule time to see someone. We try to cram too much information into a single email. We send "flaming" emails, using the medium to say things we would never say to someone in person. Personal contact, in contrast, is severely underused. We often avoid making a phone call or meeting with someone in person because we fear it will take too much time; but the misunderstandings caused by email can end up costing us far more time and sometimes frustration, conflict, or loss of productivity. (Ask participants to share examples of how all kinds of media are misused and of the communication challenges that resulted from this misuse.)

   ◆ **Message content and required response:** Be succinct. Figure out ahead of time what exactly you need to tell people or ask people and then do it. Avoid cramming multiple messages into a single communication; it's confusing. Also be clear about what response you expect from people. Do they need to acknowledge receipt of the message or verify their understanding? Are you looking for their input? Do you want them to start doing something differently? Should they contact you with questions?

(Again, ask participants to offer examples of times when this action did not occur.)

◆ **Message framing:** Context in a message can be huge. In multicultural teams, for example, not everyone will have the same meanings for words or phrases. Some phrases that are common to a North American will be meaningless to a foreign-born person. Generational differences, different work experiences, or different educational backgrounds can alter the meaning of a message. Also, don't assume that what's important to you will be important to your message recipient. Just because something is a crisis for you does not mean it's a crisis for your recipient. (Invite participants to share examples of either sending or receiving messages that did a good job of considering the recipient's field of experience. Also feel free to share an experience of your own with the group.)

◆ **Feedback mechanism:** It's dangerous to assume that people understand your messages. This is a huge problem with emails because you have no way of judging either by tone of voice or body language whether someone has understood you or even received the message. When messages are important, take time to confirm both receipt and understanding—especially when logistics are involved. Asking things such as, "What questions do you have?" when talking in person to an individual or group gives people an opportunity to verify their understanding. Better yet, ask recipients a question or two about your message's content to enable them to demonstrate their understanding of your message. When communicating via email, always ask for verification of receipt (a read receipt is *not* sufficient). Make a quick follow-up call to check in with recipients and offer them the opportunity to ask questions.

8. Divide participants into groups of three or four. Assign half the groups the topic *Communication Do's* and the other half the topic *Communication Pitfalls*.

9. Give all groups two minutes to brainstorm items related to their assigned topic. Instruct groups to write each idea on separate sticky notes.

10. While groups are writing, use flipchart pages to create four wallcharts and post them around the room. Label two wallcharts *Communication Do's* and label the other two *Communication Pitfalls*.

11. Call time after two minutes. Have group members post their ideas on the appropriate wallcharts. Ask them to bring blank sticky notes and markers with them when they gather at the charts.

12. Instruct groups to review all ideas related to their assigned topic. Then have them review the ideas generated by the teams assigned to the opposite topic. Give teams an additional two minutes to brainstorm any additional ideas they can come up with related to the new topic. This activity is a nice way to illustrate the effects of teamwork—especially as it relates to creativity and idea generation.

13. After participants have posted all ideas and reviewed the flipcharts, invite them to identify the top two or three "do's" and "pitfalls." Encourage participants to write the most important ideas on their handout.

14. Display slide 5–15. Have participants use the second page of Handout 9–10 to respond to these questions for themselves. Give one to two minutes for participants to write their responses.

15. Review the Fostering Teamwork Competency Model. Point out the behaviors associated with communication and the ideas generated by participants for being effective as well as the behaviors that can sabotage communication.

16. Make a transition to the next activity by explaining that participants will have an opportunity to test many of their ideas and figure out how to communicate with each other during a project when faced with real-world constraints.

Learning Activity 8–11: Bridge Building

Note: This learning activity is used for both the Fostering Teamwork and Developing Teamwork Skills workshops. Some questions used during the debriefing differ, depending on the workshop. The training instrument used also differs. These variations are noted within the instructions for this activity.

OBJECTIVES

The objectives of this learning activity are to

- identify and implement an effective communication strategy

- apply as many behaviors associated with demonstrating teamwork (Developing Teamwork Skills workshop) or fostering teamwork (Fostering Teamwork workshop) as possible to complete the team task on time and with the resources allocated

- overcome real-world challenges to effective communication.

MATERIALS

The materials needed for this activity are

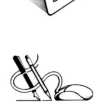

- PowerPoint slides 5–16 and 5–17 (for Fostering Teamwork workshop)

- PowerPoint slides 6–26 and 6–27 (for Developing Teamwork Skills workshop)

- Training Instrument 10–3: Bridge Building for Fostering Teamwork (only for the team leaders and the observers)

- Training Instrument 10–4: Email Communication (four or five copies for each team member)

- Training Instrument 10–5: Bridge Building for Developing Teamwork Skills (only for the team leaders and the observers)

- One flipchart, easel, and marker

- Newspapers (enough to supply teams with materials to construct a bridge that spans 2 to 3 feet of space)

- Play money ($10,000 for each team)

◆ Some type of physical barrier to separate members of the same team who are supposed to be working remotely from each other. (Team members should not have visual contact; barriers can be as simple as two chairs with a coat draped across them.)

◆ Masking tape (at least two rolls per team; if you run multiple sessions of this workshop, consider two partial rolls equal to one full role)

◆ One small object weighing five pounds (a hand weight is ideal)

◆ One shoebox that is approximately one foot long

TIME

◆ 1.75 hours (including a break)

PREPARATION

◆ Place all newspapers and rolls of masking tape at the front of the room.

◆ Create a flipchart to track each team's spending—a column for each team suffices. As teams spend money, you'll record the expenditures in the appropriate flipchart columns.

◆ Move all tables and chairs out of the center of the room. Teams need approximately 15 feet of clear floor space to do this activity. Figure 8–1 (on page 110) offers an example of the room setup.

INSTRUCTIONS

1. Group participants in teams of five, with the fifth person serving as an observer. (If the number of workshop participants can't be grouped in five-person teams, create at least two groups of four and assign the remaining people to serve as floating observers. If you have a very small group of trainees, you can place participants into groups of three and assign one or two other participants to function as observers overall.

2. Display slide 5–16 or slide 6–26 (depending on workshop) and review its contents. Give groups two to three minutes to select a team leader—ideally, someone who didn't serve as leader during the tower-building activity (Fostering Teamwork workshop) or the great-divide activity (Developing Teamwork Skills workshop).

Figure 8-1

One Suggested Room Setup for Bridge-Building Activity

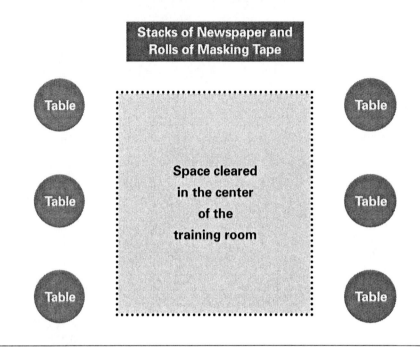

3. After teams have selected their leaders, immediately split the teams according to "geography." Send half the members of each team across the open floor space to the opposite side of the room.

4. Explain that teams are once again going to construct something, but that it is the job of the team leader to explain the task. The goal here is for participants to engage in an activity that requires an excellent communication strategy for teams to be successful in accomplishing the task.

5. Call team leaders and observers to the front of the room and do the following:

   ◆ For the Fostering Teamwork workshop, give each team leader and observer a copy of Training Instrument 10–3.

   ◆ For the Developing Teamwork Skills workshop, give each team leader and observer a copy of Training Instrument 10–5.

   ◆ Give leaders and observers time to review the contents of the instrument and ask any clarifying questions they have. Make sure observers completely understand their role. Emphasize the importance of recording their observations in the space provided on the training instrument throughout the activity so they can use them in the debriefing.

♦ Give each team leader $10,000 in play money, and copies of Training Instrument 10–4: Email Communication. Instruct them to give each team member several copies of the email form to use during the simulation. (Keep extra copies of the email form at the front of the room. Teams incur no penalty for taking extra copies.)

♦ Explain that team members are not to see the actual contents of Training Instrument 10–3 or 10–5. All information within it must be communicated face-to-face, via phone, or via email. Remind leaders and observers that the activity begins as soon as leaders return to their groups. Leaders who choose to gather the entire team into one location will incur an immediate expense of $1,000 for an onsite meeting.

♦ As team leaders or team members purchase items from the resource list, they must pay for them. You collect all money, and, on the flipchart, track how much each team spends.

6. When team leaders return to their groups, start timing the 45-minute activity. You should erect a barrier between geographically dispersed members of the same team.

7. Rotate among all groups throughout the activity and collect money as team leaders spend it. Record amounts spent as the work progresses to avoid mistakes and/or questions from the teams at the end. (Be sure to record each expense separately in each team's column. Doing so makes it easy for everyone to see which teams relied more on face-to-face, conference call, and phone communication versus the ones who relied heavily on email.) Use the observation sheet included in Training Instrument 10–5 to record your own observations of groups.

8. Give teams seven-minute, five-minute, and two-minute warnings as the time remaining decreases.

9. After 45 minutes, call time. Use the five-pound weight and the length of the shoebox to check each team's bridge. Congratulate each team that accomplished the goal. (Some teams will not.) Note the amount spent by each team. Give the appropriate "bonus" to any leader

whose team accomplished the goal for less than $10,000. Pay attention to team members' reactions when you are paying out bonuses.

10. Instruct participants to take a 10-minute break. When you reconvene, you can begin the debriefing.

DEBRIEFING

Note: Be certain you allow sufficient time to debrief this exercise fully. How much people learn from the activity depends on how well you debrief the experience with participants. It's important to allow time for all views to be heard—those of the team leaders, the team members, and observers.

1. Display slide 5–17 (Fostering Teamwork) or slide 6–27 (Developing Teamwork Skills) to identify the order in which various roles will share their insights. Review points on the slide and then invite team leaders to talk about their reactions to the communication challenge posed. Encourage them to discuss their communication decisions by using the following questions as a guide:

   ◆ What decisions did they consciously make about communication? Did they create and share a strategy about what to communicate, when to communicate, and how to communicate? Why or why not?

   ◆ How did they decide what form of communication to use?

   ◆ Which form of communication was most efficient?

   ◆ Which form of communication caused problems?

   ◆ What, if any, communication breakdowns occurred? Why did these happen?

   ◆ *Fostering Teamwork workshop*: Based on this experience, what do you think you may do differently in the workplace in communicating with your team or group members?

2. Shift the focus to team members. Invite them to share their experiences and reactions to the quality and level of communication by asking the following questions:

   ◆ Did you have input to the choices made about team communication? How did that make you feel?

♦ What forms of communication proved to be most effective?

♦ How would you rate the communication you had with your remote teammates? Were you able to work effectively with them?

♦ What form of communication did you value most?

♦ What form of communication frustrated you or hindered your ability to do your job?

♦ What forms of communication do you find yourself depending on most in the workplace? Are these the best choices?

3. Invite observers to provide additional insights based on the notes they made during the activity. Use the following questions as a guide:

♦ *Fostering Teamwork workshop:* Based on your observations during the activity, what did the leader do that was effective? What did he or she do that was ineffective or detrimental to team communication?

♦ *Fostering Teamwork workshop:* Could you describe the team leader's communication strategy (the *what, when,* and *how* of his or her communication)?

♦ What did team members do that enhanced or hindered communication?

♦ *Developing Teamwork Skills workshop:* Which key behaviors did you see people demonstrate? Give examples. Which key behaviors were missing? How might these have helped?

4. If your own observation notes contain points that participants have not already made, mention them now. Focus your comments on what you saw the leader and members doing well or poorly and the impact you observed it having on the team's ability to get the task done, the environment in which team members were working, and the degree of collaboration occurring among team members. For the Developing Teamwork Skills workshop, place less emphasis on the leader's behaviors and focus instead on the team members' behaviors.

5. *Fostering Teamwork workshop:* After discussing communication strategy, debrief the other observations made about how team leaders fostered teamwork. Invite leaders, then team members, and finally observers to respond to these questions:

◆ How effective overall was the team leader at fostering teamwork throughout the experience? What behaviors did she or he do well? What behaviors were absent? (Encourage observers, in particular, to be specific about the behaviors they saw that related to the Fostering Teamwork Competency Model.)

◆ What could the team leader have done differently to produce a better result?

◆ Did the team leader let members know of the potential bonus? If yes, how was this handled? Did the team leader offer to share the bonus? If the team leader did not, how did members feel about working to give a team leader a bonus they would not share? If the team leader did *not* let members know about the potential bonus, how did members feel when they saw the leader being rewarded? In the real world, what effect would this type of incentive structure have on team or group members?

6. Create a flipchart page labeled *Lessons Learned.* Invite participants to identify the most important lessons learned from the activity. Write down responses and post on the wall for everyone to see. (For the Fostering Teamwork workshop, focus lessons learned on the fostering teamwork competency. For the Developing Teamwork Skills workshop, focus lessons learned on the demonstrating teamwork competency.)

7. Acknowledge everyone's efforts in participating and sharing ideas. Thank them for their work.

Learning Activity 8-12:
Decisions and Other Roadblocks

OBJECTIVES

The objectives of this learning activity are to

- recognize common roadblocks that hinder a team or group's ability to accomplish tasks

- identify the role of a team leader or a manager in addressing roadblocks

- use an accountability matrix as a decision-making tool.

MATERIALS

The materials needed for this activity are

- PowerPoint slides 5–18 through 5–21

- Handout 9–9: Decisions and Other Roadblocks

- One or two pieces of flipchart paper and two or three markers for each team

TIME

- 30 minutes

PREPARATION

- None

INSTRUCTIONS

1. Display slide 5–18. Explain that a *roadblock* refers to anything that makes it tough for a team to do its work. Roadblocks could include lack of resources, an insufficient timeline, lack of expertise, and so forth. Roadblocks are commonly things that team members can't remove by themselves. They need assistance from the team leader. Poor decision-making abilities on a team thus become another type of roadblock. It's up to the team leader to establish some sort of decision-making process—or to lead the team in deciding on one—so that

when disagreements and problems arise, the team has a way of coming to a decision about what to do.

2. Distribute blank flipchart pages and markers to each team that completed the bridge-building scenario. Direct learners' attention to Handout 9–9. Display slide 5–19 and review the instructions. Give teams seven minutes to brainstorm ideas. If necessary, provide them with additional sheets of flipchart paper to record their ideas.

3. At the end of seven minutes, call time. Have each team share its responses to the questions. As teams list their roadblocks and decision points, make sure you note commonalities among groups and among leaders' responses to situations. Probe for clarification on a team's assessment regarding the team leader's effectiveness and ineffectiveness. Make sure all groups explain their rationales for rating the leaders as they did. When two teams encountered the same roadblock or decision, but team leaders responded differently, make note of that as well. Encourage the group to discuss what made one leader's approach more or less effective than another leader's approach.

4. Emphasize that although a team leader may not have expertise in everything that the team does, he or she should have skill in removing roadblocks and facilitating decision making. Failing to establish some sort of decision-making framework is a trap many team leaders fall into. They either default to making all decisions themselves (which is inefficient, slow, and annoying to team members) or they fail to establish *any* decision-making criteria, which confuses team members and bogs processes down.

5. Display slide 5–20. Explain the purpose of an accountability chart and how it can improve team efficiency. By deciding ahead of time who makes what types of decisions, teams can avoid paralysis when a problem arises. Decision makers will vary with the type of situation encountered. Financial decisions may always default to the team leader. Process decisions may rotate, depending on the expertise of different team members. In the bridge-building activity, one person may have been designated as the design expert. This person nay have then had final decision-making responsibility on the amount of material required. The team leader, who was responsible for the budget, needed to be informed of material requirements. If the required materials exceeded the team's budget, then the team leader

may have advised the design expert that an alternate design would need to be considered.

6. Review the accountability chart example included in Handout 9–9. Invite participants to comment on the decision categories and the roles assigned. Ask the following questions:

 ♦ What other roles could be defined for this team effort?

 ♦ What other types of decision categories could be included?

 ♦ Would such a chart be helpful—especially on larger, more complex efforts?

 ♦ Can you give an example of how you might use such a chart in your workplace?

7. Display slide 5–21. Briefly discuss roadblocks that the team itself could not address—perhaps a lack of resources, time, or money. These are true roadblocks to the team. They cannot remove the barriers themselves. When a team finds itself spending lots of time discussing a problem, the first question the team leader and team members need to ask is, "Can we make this decision and/or solve this problem?" When the answer is *no*, the issue immediately gets tabled. The team leader becomes responsible for removing the roadblock by taking the issue to the appropriate decision maker (perhaps a stakeholder or the team leader's manager). The team leader also needs to coach members in this process. The leader will not be attending every meeting or communication exchange between team members. When members hit a roadblock, they need to table the issue and take it to the team leader for resolution. This process keeps teams from spending large amounts of time discussing issues they lack the ability to resolve.

8. Conclude the discussion by asking participants what questions they have. Refer to the Fostering Teamwork Competency Model and point out where decision making and removing roadblocks appear as key behaviors.

Learning Activity 8–13:
Learning Recap #2

OBJECTIVE

The objective of this learning activity is to identify personal learning achievement and plan application in the workplace.

MATERIALS

The materials needed for this activity are

- ◆   Handout 9–8: Learning Recaps (distributed earlier in the workshop)

- ◆   PowerPoint slide 5–22 (Fostering Teamwork workshop)

- ◆   PowerPoint slide 6–28 (Developing Teamwork Skills workshop)

TIME

- ◆   15 minutes

PREPARATION

- ◆   None

INSTRUCTIONS

1.   Display PowerPoint slide 5–22 (Fostering Teamwork workshop) or slide 6–28 (Developing Teamwork Skills workshop).

2.   Refer participants to Handout 9–8: Learning Recaps, which you distributed to them in the morning.

3.   Explain that participants should take time to review their behavior self-assessment and think about the activities and discussion that have occurred this afternoon.

4.   Ask them to identify key learning points that relate to their behavior self-assessment and identify one to three actions they can take in the workplace to improve their ability to foster teamwork.

5.   If time permits, consider asking participants to share their key learning points and proposed actions. As an option, you may have participants select a partner and share this information with each other.

6. After participants share their thoughts, refer to the agenda for the day and either the Fostering Teamwork or the Demonstrating Teamwork Competency Model (which you posted on the wall at the start of the workshop).

7. Summarize the learning and activities that occurred throughout the day. Point out how the team-building exercises (tower building and bridge building for Fostering Teamwork workshop and crossing the great divide and bridge building for Developing Teamwork Skills workshop) enabled participants to experience the role these key behaviors play in fostering teamwork or developing teamwork skills— either because team leaders or team members demonstrated these behaviors or because they failed to demonstrate the behaviors. In each scenario there was a consequence. Review the definition and key behaviors associated with the competency of fostering teamwork or demonstrating teamwork one final time.

Learning Activity 8–14:
What Is Teamwork, and What Is Its Value?

OBJECTIVES

The objectives of this learning activity are to

- define and describe teamwork

- identify ways in which teamwork adds value to the organization and to the people who work within it.

MATERIALS

The materials needed for this activity are

- Assessment 10–3: Am I a Team Player? (This is pre-work. Participants should be sent this document prior to the workshop with instructions to bring the completed assessment to the session.)

- PowerPoint slides 6–4 through 6–7

- Yellow, green, and red sticky dots

- A flipchart page labeled *Parking Lot*

- Masking tape or pushpins for hanging flipchart pages

- One or two pads of 4x6-inch sticky notes and markers for every three to four people in the room

- Wallchart showing the competency model for Demonstrating Teamwork (the first table in Handout 9–2)

TIME

- 30 minutes

PREPARATION

- Enlarge the Am I a Team Player assessment and the Demonstrating Teamwork Competency Model into wallcharts. Hang the enlarged versions on the walls of the training room.

- Make sure each participant is sent Assessment 10–3 as part of her or his pre-work assignment. In any advance communication with participants, stress the importance of completing this tool prior to attending the session.

◆ Create a Parking Lot by labeling a flipchart page with that title and posting it on the wall where participants can see and reach it easily.

◆ Place pads of sticky notes and markers on each table for participants' use during the session.

INSTRUCTIONS

1. Display slide 6–4 as a "marker" to indicate the segment of the workshop you are covering.

2. Explain the Parking Lot flipchart. Indicate that during this activity—and throughout the entire day—participants may have questions or issues that are outside the scope of this training session. When such questions or issues arise, learners can write them on a sticky note and place them on the Parking Lot page. They will be addressed by you outside the workshop or at the appropriate time during the workshop. They will be tabled, but not forgotten. (**Note:** It's important that you have a plan for addressing items that are posted on the Parking Lot. Some of the issues may relate to concerns about managers' ability to foster teamwork. Be prepared!) If items are addressed during the workshop, remove them from the Parking Lot.

3. Direct participants' attention to Handout 9–2. Explain that this handout defines the competency of demonstrating teamwork. It also identifies the key behaviors associated with the competency. The model is research based. The assessment participants completed prior to the training session is based on this model.

4. Display slide 6–5. Explain that this model identifies behaviors required to demonstrate teamwork, but if the employees who work for the organization are to demonstrate teamwork, they need to buy into its value to themselves and the organization. Ask participants the following questions, and be prepared to share your own examples if participants struggle to get started. Allow several participants to respond to each question. The goal of these questions is to help participants establish a reason *why* they should care about teamwork and what behaviors really make someone effective as a team player. Here are the questions:

- **What value does teamwork have in organizations?** (Possible responses: *Getting tasks done faster, getting better-quality ideas or problem solving, bringing together expertise that simply doesn't reside in any one person, accomplishing goals that a person working alone could not accomplish*)

- **Why is teamwork important within this organization?** (Participants will have a variety of responses, but probe for some specific examples, such as *because it reduces our time to market with a new product, because it gives us a competitive advantage, because it saves us x dollars in manufacturing costs.*)

- **What examples from within your own work experience demonstrate the value teamwork can have for you and for others?** (Encourage participants to be thoughtful in their responses to this question. Prompt people to share stories of how teamwork accomplished a goal that individuals could not have done by themselves.)

- **What behaviors do you think are most critical for being an effective team player?** Look for agreement with the behaviors displayed on the competency model and within the self-assessment. As participants identify behaviors, be sure to point out the ones that mirror those listed in the competency model. Be prepared for participants to point out that these behaviors only occur if they are supported by leaders and management. At that point, you can direct concerns such as these to the Parking Lot flipchart.

5. Acknowledge participants' efforts at responding to the questions—especially the last one. Explain that the self-assessment that attendees took prior to the session can help them identify how well they function as a team player and where they have opportunities to improve.

6. Display slide 6–6. Direct participants to use their yellow, red, and green dots to mark their assessments according to the directions on slide 6–5. Participants are to use their green dots to mark their **yes** responses, the red dots to mark **no** responses, and the yellow dots to mark **not sure** responses.

7. Divide participants into groups of three to four people. Display slide 6–7 and have groups follow the directions on the slide. Provide each

group with a supply of red and green dots. Have them mark the chart based on their group discussion.

DEBRIEFING

1. Review the results on the flipchart. Point out the areas of strength (consensus *yes* response) within the entire training group (if any). Invite participants to share examples of what they have done as team members that causes them to rate these as *yes* responses. (Do this to make sure that participants can support their *yes* responses.)

2. Shift the focus to the *areas of opportunity* responses (red dots). Ask participants to share why these items were rated as areas of opportunity for the group. Ask participants to identify the potential ramifications if these areas are not developed. Point out that any failing to do any of the behaviors listed in the self-assessment can sabotage someone's ability to operate effectively as a team player.

3. Thank participants for compiling results. Indicate that the remainder of the day will be spent developing skills that are identified in the self-assessment and the competency model. Note that because attendees may have different developmental needs, the activities are designed to promote the development of multiple skills.

Learning Activity 8–15:
Effective Communication—
The Foundation of Teamwork

OBJECTIVES

The objectives of this learning activity are to

- identify listening and speaking behaviors that enhance or that hinder teamwork

- improve skills in listening, sharing ideas, and giving and receiving feedback.

MATERIALS

The materials needed for this activity are

- Training Instrument 10–6: Listening Assessment (one copy for each participant)

- Handout 9–11: Effective Communication—The Foundation to Demonstrating Teamwork (one copy for each participant)

- PowerPoint slides 6–8 through 6–22

- A flipchart pad and easel, and various colored markers

- Masking tape or pushpins for attaching flipchart pages to the wall

TIME

- 1.5 hours

PREPARATION

- None

INSTRUCTIONS

1. Display slide 6–8 as a "marker" to indicate the segment of the workshop you are covering.

2. Explain that listening, sharing ideas, and exchanging feedback are cornerstone skills for a team player. It's difficult to be effective within a team if you can't demonstrate these skills consistently. For the

next 1.5 hours, participants are going to evaluate their skills in these basic areas and practice improving the skills.

Part 1: Are You Listening or Just Waiting to Talk?

3. Distribute Training Instrument 10–6 and display slide 6–9. Have participants complete the assessment according to the directions on the slide. Give them five to seven minutes to complete the assessment *two times* and to calculate their scores. Poll the group to find out how they scored. (The majority will probably have 10 or fewer correct responses.) Also poll the group to find out how many of them had lower scores when they took the assessment the second time. (Most will.) Make the point that when we are really honest about our behaviors, most of us have multiple opportunities to improve our behaviors as listeners.

4. Display slide 6–10 and distribute Handout 9–11. Explain that the handout is for participants to use in notetaking during large- and small-group discussions.

5. Create two flipcharts. Label one "Listening Faux Pas" and the other "Listening Virtues." Invite the group to identify the biggest faux pas (mistakes) that people make when listening and the biggest virtues listeners can demonstrate. Display slides 6–11 and 6–12 and compare learners' responses with the ones on the slides.

6. Have each participant team with another person. Display slide 6–13 and let participants know they are going to practice both the sins and the virtues. As described on the slide, one person in the dyad is to be the speaker; the other is to be the listener. The speaker is to talk on a topic of his or her choice for 90 seconds; the listener is to commit as many of the seven listening sins as possible during those 90 seconds. Instruct pairs to begin.

7. After 90 seconds, call time. Invite several of the speakers to describe their reactions to the experience. Probe to find out how the listeners' behaviors affected their ability to share their ideas—or even to get feedback on what they were saying. The general response should be that the poor listening behaviors made it very difficult to share information.

8. Instruct pairs to repeat the exercise. This time the listener is to practice as many of the seven virtues as possible. Instruct pairs to begin.

9. After 90 seconds, call time. Again invite several speakers to describe their reactions to the experience. Most people will probably indicate they found it much easier and more enjoyable to share. The partners' good listening behaviors encouraged idea exchange and positive body language offered a form of positive feedback.

Part II: It's Not Just What You Say

10. Display slide 6–14. Segue into the idea-sharing portion of this topic by pointing out that idea-sharing or idea presentation involves more than words.

11. Display slide 6–15. Ask two volunteers to stand and say each phrase listed on the slide. However, each person is to convey a different meaning for each phrase. After each phrase is stated, invite the audience to guess the true meaning being expressed. (For example, the sentence "It's a nice dress" can be stated so that it really means the opposite or in a way that the person hearing the sentence is unsure of the speaker's true meaning.)

12. Display slide 6–16 and review the information. Point out that because more than 60 percent of the message being delivered is expressed nonverbally, it's important that people are aware of unintentional messages they may be sending. Body movement, tone of voice, rate of speech, facial expressions, and gestures all send messages right along with the words. If a speaker isn't careful, the nonverbal message can cancel out or change the meaning of the verbal one!

13. Display slide 6–17 and review its information. Key points to make include the following:

- Positive language works much better than negative language. Rather than focusing on what cannot be done, focus on what can be done. Rather than stating something will not work, express yourself in terms of what will or may work. Rather than telling people what not to do, tell them what *to do.*

- Pictures speak so much louder than words alone that when you are forced to only use words, you need to select words that are specific and descriptive. Try to paint a picture with words—otherwise, your listener will try to paint her or his own picture. Use specific examples to illustrate meaning and to help the listener understand your viewpoint.

14. Display slide 6–18 and invite participants to practice using these concepts. Possible answers for each sentence are listed below:

- I don't think your idea will work: *Help me understand how your idea will work,* or *I have some concerns about your idea. Can you explain...?* or *What will it take to make your idea work?*

- We don't need another meeting: *Why do you think we need another meeting?* or *What do you want to accomplish with another meeting?* or *I'd really like to avoid another meeting if it's possible because....*

- We can't have this ready by Friday: *I have these five tasks to complete by Friday. What should my priority be?* or *Here are the ramifications if we push to get this done by Friday.*

- It's cold out: *It's so cold outside that my hands have gone numb and I have icicles on my lashes.*

- You did a nice job: *You responded to all questions during the meeting, you stuck to the timeline, and you came prepared with facts.*

- Your report looks good: *I really liked your report. You used lots of examples, which helped me understand your viewpoint. You also cited several statistics to support your analysis. Finally, you created a concise executive summary.*

- You did a poor job: *Your effort did not meet expectations. You were not prepared to address questions, you went over the allotted time, and you did not have the facts to support your presentation.*

15. Display slide 6–19 and review its contents. Key points to make include the following:

- By using your eyes, your voice, and gestures you can help focus the listener and maintain his or her interest. When you fail to make contact and fail to use your voice (volume, pitch, and rate of speed), you miss out on chances to be more effective. (**Note:** Consider demonstrating how someone can be effective or ineffective with eye contact, voice, and gestures.)

- Purposeful movement can help focus your listener as well. Physically moving as you make different points helps give listeners a visual cue to go along with your verbal cues. (Example: *My first point is....* At conclusion of the first point, move to a new spot and say, *My second point is....* At conclusion of the second point, move to a third spot and say, *My final point is....*)

16. Display slide 6–20 and have participants form groups of three or four. (If you have a group of four, then have two people function as observers instead of one person doing so.) Explain that this activity provides learners with an opportunity to apply the listening and speaking skills discussed. Each person will have a turn at the role of speaker while the others function as listeners. Each speaker is to spend 60 seconds explaining her or his opinion of the most important attribute of a team player. Listeners should demonstrate listening virtues; speakers should practice the techniques just discussed.

17. Direct groups to begin. Call time after 60 seconds and have participants switch roles. Repeat enough times so all members have the opportunity to practice being the speaker.

18. After all rounds have concluded, invite participants to discuss their experience. Elicit what participants found hardest and easiest to do as a speaker. What tips discussed in class really helped them as they shared their ideas? What would they still like to improve?

19. Depending on how much time has elapsed, you may want to call for a 10-minute break.

Part III: Email

20. Display slide 6–21. Explain that email is a major part of team communications in today's work environments. Many people receive 100+ emails each day. Sending and responding to emails can be a huge challenge—one that causes people many problems. Team communication can either be enhanced or hindered by how people use and misuse email.

21. Review the list of what to do and what not to do on slides 6–21 and 6–22. Invite participants to comment on how email has enhanced or hindered their team communication. Write participants' responses on a flipchart page and hang it on wall.

22. Summarize this learning activity by reemphasizing the importance of listening and idea-sharing skills among team players. Lack of clarity on a team's goal is the number-one reason that teams fail. The second reason relates to communication and trust, which are interrelated. One way in which you build trust is through effective communication.

Learning Activity 8–16:
Crossing the Great Divide

OBJECTIVES

The objectives of this learning activity are to

- apply skills and behaviors discussed thus far that are related to listening, sharing ideas, creating a positive environment, and building trust

- resolve conflicts that emerge during the activity.

MATERIALS

The materials needed for this activity are

- Masking tape

- PowerPoint slide 6–25

- Flipchart easel and a pad of paper, and markers of various colors

TIME

- 30 minutes

PREPARATION

- Place two lines of masking tape on the floor, approximately 10 to 12 feet apart. The tape lines should be long enough for everyone in the room to stand comfortably along a line in groups of five to seven people. If you have the space, you may want to create a separate "divide" for each group of five to seven people. See figure 8–2 on page 130.

INSTRUCTIONS

1. Explain that participants are going to take part in a team-building exercise. Their objective is to apply the skills and behaviors discussed in the morning to this brief team-building activity.

2. Select one or two people to function as observers. Divide the remaining participants into teams of five to seven people.

Figure 8–2

Layout for the Great Divide

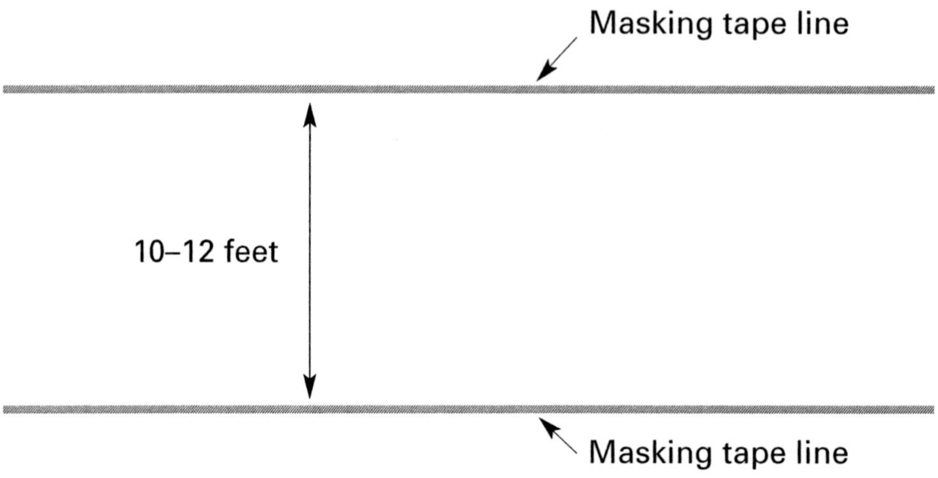

Masking tape line

10–12 feet

Masking tape line

---

3. Display slide 6–25. Have participants line up along one of the masking tape lines that mark the "Great Divide." Explain that the outside edges of their feet should be touching each other as they stand along the line. See figure 8–3. Groups can do this activity simultaneously, but you'll need an observer for each group.

4. Assign one person in each group the role of team leader; all others are to function as team members. The team leader's role is to make sure that everyone's ideas are heard and the team makes progress toward its goal.

Figure 8–3

Foot Placement for a Five-Person Team in the Great Divide

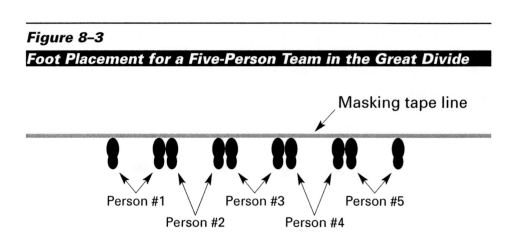

Masking tape line

Person #1   Person #3   Person #5

Person #2   Person #4

5. Explain that teams are to cross the divide without breaking contact with their feet. Encourage them to plan out how this task will be accomplished before they actually start moving. Make sure that all teams understand their goal, and then direct them to begin.

6. During this activity, observers are to watch closely to make sure teams' feet don't break contact. Whenever they do break contact, observers are to send the entire team back to the starting line to begin again. (**Note:** Some teams may get quite frustrated if they have to return to the starting point multiple times.) Observers are also to watch how team members listen to each other, share ideas, and build trust within their team. Your job is to make the same observations.

7. Call time when the majority of teams have successfully crossed the Great Divide. Invite everyone to return to their seats for the debriefing.

DEBRIEFING

1. Use the flipchart to record participants' and observers' answers to the following questions. Have observers respond to each question separately from the participants before participants respond:

   ◆ **What challenges did you encounter in this activity?** (Communication should be cited, as should staying focused and organized. People probably had difficulty being heard. They may also have engaged in multiple side conversations with the people immediately next to them. The team leader may or may not have been open to hearing ideas. Conflict may also have erupted if the team found itself returning to the starting line several times.)

   ◆ **How are the challenges you encountered with this experience similar to ones you've had working with members of your work teams or groups?** (Most people will probably talk about struggles with listening to others, difficulty in getting their ideas across, or frustrations with team members. A few may also mention the team leader's role in enhancing or hindering team communication and focus.)

   ◆ **What did you learn about working within a team while doing this exercise?** (Answers will vary. See if people will talk about the challenge of maintaining good communication and good listening behaviors when frustration increases. Also try to elicit people's trust issues—did they trust their teammates to come up with good solutions to the problem or did they want to rely on themselves?)

◆ **What would have made your team(s) more successful in this task?** (Answers will vary, but people will probably mention better planning as well as hearing all possible ideas before pursuing a course of action. They may also mention the team leader's need to consider multiple points of view before taking action. Point out that effective listening and idea-sharing behaviors can help a great deal in this area.)

2. Thank participants and observers for their efforts during the exercise as well as their ideas following the exercise.

3. Post all flipchart pages where participants can view them during the next exercise.

◆ ◆ ◆

Coming in the next chapter are the handouts that the teamwork training workshops incorporate. You'll print copies of these materials (customizing them as you wish to fit your organization's needs) and distribute them to your learners.

Handouts

What's in This Chapter?

- ◆ Eleven handouts to enhance the learning experience for workshop participants and extend the learning when participants are back on the job

This chapter contains all of the handouts associated with the three workshops that are part of this book. You will notice that some handouts are used in more than one workshop; others are used in only one of the three workshops. The term *handout* means that the item is something you copy and distribute to all participants for their use during the workshop. Handouts differ from the other resources provided in the workbook: pre-work (the assessments), those materials given to only one or several participants during the workshop (training instruments), or items simply intended to be an aid for your use (tools).

Electronic versions of the handouts are located on the CD in the file folder labeled "Handouts." For easy reference, the file naming convention follows the labels used in this book (that is, Handout 9–1, Handout 9–2, and so forth). When you select handouts for a particular workshop, you may want to rename them and sequence them with a simple numbering system that reflects the order in which your learners will use them.

Handout 9–1

Executive Overview Objectives and Agenda

Objectives

- Describe the benefits of effective teamwork, the factors that contribute to it, and the factors that hinder its development and implementation

- Evaluate the current level of teamwork occurring within the organization

- Identify the role of the executive leaders in promoting and supporting teamwork throughout the organization

- Define the competencies for fostering and for demonstrating teamwork and identify the key behaviors taught in the teamwork workshops

Agenda

8:30 a.m.	Welcome and introductions
8:40	Session objectives and agenda
8:45	Reviewing the organizational teamwork assessment results
9:15	Creating a climate that supports teamwork
9:45	Reviewing what's covered in the teamwork workshops
10:00	End of session

Handout 9–2

Teamwork Competency Models

A Competency Model for Demonstrating Teamwork

COMPETENCY DEFINITION	KEY BEHAVIORS
The ability to work cooperatively and/or collaboratively with others in pursuit of a common goal	<ul><li>Listen and respond constructively to other group or team members' ideas</li><li>Share one's own ideas with the group</li><li>Openly express any concerns to other team or group members</li><li>Acknowledge when conflict exists and express disagreement constructively</li><li>Give honest and constructive feedback to other team members</li><li>Provide assistance to other team members, group members, or work units when needed</li><li>Work toward solutions that all members of the team or group can support; support team or group decisions</li><li>Share professional expertise with others</li></ul>

continued on next page

Handout 9–2, continued

Teamwork Competency Models

A Competency Model for Fostering Teamwork

COMPETENCY DEFINITION	KEY BEHAVIORS

The ability to encourage and enable others to work cooperatively and/or collaboratively toward a goal	◆ Promote and gain buy-in and agreement on a common mission and goal
	
	◆ Reinforce mission or goal on an ongoing basis
	
	◆ Clarify roles, responsibilities, and accountabilities
	
	◆ Promote cooperation with other work groups or units
	
	◆ Establish and implement a communication framework
	
	◆ Create an environment that reinforces teamwork:
	
	  ◆ structure rewards and incentives to reinforce collaboration
	
	  ◆ create an atmosphere that encourages collaboration instead of competition
	
	  ◆ provide opportunities for people to learn how to work together
	
	  ◆ cultivate trust among team members
	
	◆ Identify and remove roadblocks that cannot be handled at the team level
	
	◆ Recognize the behaviors that contribute to teamwork; coach the team and individuals within the team on these behaviors
	
	◆ Establish and implement team decision-making and problem-solving processes

Handout 9–3
Improving the Organizational Climate

Instructions: As a management group, review the results of the organizational teamwork assessment. Document all items that need to be addressed, what action to take, who is responsible, and when action should occur.

ITEM TO ADDRESS	ACTION TO TAKE	PERSON ACCOUNTABLE	TARGET DATE FOR IMPLEMENTATION

Handout 9–4

Fostering Teamwork Workshop Objectives and Agenda

Objectives

- ◆ Describe the benefits of effective teamwork, the factors that contribute to it, and the factors that hinder its development and implementation

- ◆ Evaluate the current level of teamwork occurring within your team, work group, or department

- ◆ Define the competency *Fostering Teamwork* and identify the key behaviors associated with it

- ◆ Assess your skill level in fostering teamwork and identify the behaviors most in need of development

- ◆ Improve your skill in fostering teamwork through use of simulation team experiences

- ◆ Develop an action plan for transferring skills to the job

Agenda

15 minutes	Welcome, introductions, and workshop overview
30 minutes	What is teamwork and is it happening where you are?
35 minutes	Team exercise: Tower Building, Part 1
10 minutes	Break
25 minutes	Team exercise: Tower Building, Part 2
30 minutes	Trust builders and trust destroyers
25 minutes	Teamwork war story: A matter of trust
20 minutes	Learning recap #1 and summary of the morning's activities
60 minutes	Lunch break
40 minutes	Communication challenges
5 minutes	Mini-break
105 minutes	Team exercise: Bridge-building challenge (includes a break)
30 minutes	Decisions and other roadblocks
15 minutes	Learning recap #2 and summary of the afternoon's activities
5 minutes	Workshop wrap-up and evaluation

Note: Times are approximate. Some activities may require slightly more or less time, depending on the number of participants in the workshop.

Handout 9–5

Developing Teamwork Skills Workshop Objectives and Agenda

Objectives

- ◆ Define the competency *Demonstrates Teamwork* and identify the key behaviors associated with it

- ◆ Describe the benefits of effective teamwork, and the ways team members or group members contribute to or hinder the practice of teamwork

- ◆ Assess your skill level in demonstrating teamwork and identify the behaviors most in need of development

- ◆ Improve your skills in listening, sharing ideas, giving and receiving feedback, and working through conflict during team and group activities

- ◆ Develop an action plan for transferring skills to the job

Agenda

15 minutes	Welcome, introductions, and workshop overview
30 minutes	What is teamwork and what is its value?
90 minutes	Effective communication: The foundation of teamwork (includes a break)
10 minutes	Break
30 minutes	Trust builders and trust destroyers
15 minutes	Learning recap #1 and summary of the morning's activities
60 minutes	Lunch break
30 minutes	Crossing the great divide
105 minutes	Bridge-building challenge
15 minutes	Learning recap #2 and summary of the afternoon's activities
5 minutes	Workshop conclusion

Note: Times are approximate. Some activities may require slightly more or less time, depending on the number of participants in the class.

Handout 9–6
Teamwork War Story—A Matter of Trust

Instructions: Read the following story silently, and then discuss it as a group. Decide what action(s) you think the team leader characterized in the story should take.

Susan owns a small consulting firm. Her employee, Jane, is managing a medium-size project for one of the firm's clients. For this project, Susan is mentoring and providing support to Jane. On other projects, Susan assumes the lead role and Jane provides specific expertise. Sometimes the project team is composed of only Susan and Jane, but at other times, teams have several members.

The project on which Jane is taking the lead now centers on developing three different products or deliverables for the company. Two of the deliverables are competency models for two different employee roles within the client company; the third deliverable is a findings/recommendations report that identifies skill and knowledge gaps in these two employee groups and recommends a curriculum design for closing these gaps.

This is the first time Jane has developed competency models or created a curriculum design, which is why Susan is mentoring her. The project plan is based on a proposal Susan's company submitted; it follows an agreed-upon statement of work.

With minimal guidance from Susan, Jane has done an excellent job creating the first two deliverables, and the client company has indicated it is extremely pleased with her work. Susan is also pleased; she sees that Jane has worked hard and is satisfying the client. For the most part, Susan leaves Jane alone with the project—only offering advice when Jane requests it, although she does review each deliverable before the client sees it.

Before Jane writes the findings/recommendations report, she sits down with the client and discusses what she plans to include in it. The client company's project manager indicates she is supportive of Jane's ideas. When Jane shares her thoughts on the report with Susan, Susan expresses some concern that the recommendations Jane plans to make may be too high-level. She has assumed that more detail would be needed, along with more analysis of the client's existing training offerings. Jane assures her the client has agreed with all recommendations, and this is the level of detail the client expects. Had Susan been doing the project, she knows she would have delivered a different level of detail, but she does not want to micromanage Jane or show a lack of trust in her expertise.

Jane spends hours creating this report. Susan reviews and approves it to go to the client on the basis of Jane's assertions that it's what the client expects to see. Shortly after receiving the report, the client calls to set up a meeting. She

continued on next page

Handout 9–6, continued

Teamwork War Story—A Matter of Trust

indicates on the phone that the reviewers are not happy with the report. In fact, the client team has serious concerns. Both Susan and Jane agree to participate in a phone conference to discuss these concerns.

During the phone conference, the client team expresses great dissatisfaction with the report and with Jane's analysis efforts. They question the report's quality and the amount of time that went into preparing it ("It appears that not more than one or two hours went into creating this document," one team member says, and the others agree.) They refer to the original contract with Susan's company, and indicate they feel that the report does not meet contractual requirements.

What should Susan do? How will her actions help or hinder teamwork within her organization, specifically in the area of cultivating trust?

_____

_____

_____

_____

_____

_____

_____

_____

_____

Handout 9–7
Teamwork War Story—What Really Happened

During the client phone call involving all parties (including Jane), Susan maintained her support of Jane. Although she expressed regret that the report missed the client's expectations, she never blamed Jane for any shortcomings the client perceived to exist in the report. Instead, she spoke in support of Jane's efforts.

When one person on the client company's team said that the report could have taken only "one to two hours," Susan calmly said she regretted that it appeared that way because she knew Jane had put many hours into writing the report. She also noted that Jane had met with the client's project manager and told her what the contents would be before she wrote anything. When the client responded that the client team assumed there would be additional information in the report, Susan went into problem-solving mode and asked the client what additional material was expected and what needed to happen to make the report meet their needs.

After the phone conference, Susan talked with Jane, who was quite upset about the situation. She asked Jane to offer her perspective about what happened. She listened to Jane, and together they agreed on a plan for moving forward. The two jointly agreed that they should work together to do additional analysis and then rewrite the findings and recommendations.

Susan set up a meeting so she and Jane could work together on outlining a new report structure. She helped Jane do some more detailed analysis, but she didn't do all the analysis or rewriting work herself.

Susan had Jane resubmit the report and then continue to work with the client, thereby letting Jane know that she still trusted her to manage the client relationship effectively. The revamped report exceeded the client's expectations and met with overwhelming positive remarks. The project manager invited Susan and Jane to present the report to a full committee and offered recognition to them for the outstanding work.

Afterward, Susan and Jane discussed what Jane had done well on the project and what she could do differently in a future project. Susan also discussed what she herself would do differently in the future and invited Jane to give her feedback as well.

The bottom line: The key thing Susan did to foster teamwork was to use the situation to help cultivate an atmosphere of trust. She didn't blame Jane or allow her to take the "rap" from the client for the unsatisfactory work. She also modeled teamwork with Jane by collaborating with her to resolve the problem rather than expecting Jane to fix the problem herself, and she didn't take over the project or shut Jane out of the process. Finally, she actively recognized Jane's efforts and used the opportunity as a coaching situation.

Note: This story is true, but the names have been changed to protect the privacy of the individuals involved.

Handout 9–8

Learning Recaps

Objectives

- Identify key learning points throughout the course
- Create an action plan for implementing what has been learned in the workshop

Learning Recap #1

LEARNING POINTS	SPECIFIC SITUATIONS WHERE I CAN APPLY THIS TO MY WORKPLACE
1.	
2.	
3.	

Learning Recap #2

LEARNING POINTS	SPECIFIC SITUATIONS WHERE I CAN APPLY THIS TO MY WORKPLACE
1.	
2.	
3.	

Handout 9–9

Decisions and Other Roadblocks

Objectives

- ♦ Recognize common roadblocks that hinder a team's or group's ability to accomplish tasks

- ♦ Identify the role of a team leader or manager in addressing roadblocks

- ♦ Use an accountability matrix as a decision-making tool

Team Activity: Identify Roadblocks and Decision Points

1. As a team, brainstorm to create a list of roadblocks and decisions your team encountered during the bridge-building simulation. Using the flipchart provided, create a chart that looks like the one depicted in the following figure—a T chart.

Roadblocks Encountered	Leader's Response
Decisions to Make	Process Used

2. Decide how effective or ineffective you believe the team leader was in addressing roadblocks and facilitating decision making within the group. Avoid the temptation to be "kind" to the participants who served as leaders during the simulation. Be honest in your assessments, and be objective. Regardless of whether you label the leader's actions as effective or ineffective, be prepared to explain why you rated the leader's actions as you did.

continued on next page

Handout 9–9, continued

Decisions and Other Roadblocks

Large-Group Activity: Create an Accountability Chart for Decision Making

The bridge-building simulation is a relatively simple exercise of short duration, so creating an accountability chart may seem like overkill. In the real work world, however, decision making frequently bogs teams down. Creating such a chart can give a team a valuable structure to turn to when a tough decision or conflict emerges. Remember, the team leader or the manager should *not* make every decision. If that is what's happening, then the team is really not functioning effectively.

An accountability chart establishes major decision categories and then identifies what role is accountable for making each type of decision. Only one role makes the decision, although one or more other roles may provide expertise to assist the decision maker. Examples of roles that people performed for the bridge-building activity could include

◆ project sponsor (facilitator)

◆ project manager (team leader)

◆ engineer(s) (whoever helped design the bridge)

◆ construction manager or construction workers.

When you've taken time to define the roles, filling in the chart becomes easier. As you quickly can see, the team leader may end up being consulted on some decisions and merely informed of others. Few decisions ultimately have to be made by the team leader, although the leader may facilitate discussions that enable others to reach decisions.

A sample chart for the bridge-building activity could look like this (**note:** this is not a "correct" answer, but a possible scenario; the team may have valid reasons for assigning roles differently):

TYPE OF DECISION	ACCOUNTABLE	CONSULTED	INFORMED
Bridge design	Engineer	Construction manager	Team leader
Resource acquisition	Construction manager	Engineer, team leader	Construction workers
Logistics	Team leader		Engineer, construction manager or workers
Construction	Construction manager	Engineer	Team leader
Financing	Team leader	Engineer, construction manager	

Notes on Removing Roadblocks and on Decision-Making Tactics

_____

_____

_____

Handout 9–10

Recognizing and Overcoming Communication Challenges

Objectives

- ◆ Define "effective" communication
- ◆ Describe the effects that good and poor personal communication have on members of a team and on the overall team environment
- ◆ Identify personal communication behaviors and tools that enhance and that hinder effective communication

Your definition of effective communication:

_____

_____

_____

_____

_____

Other participants' definitions and ideas about effective communication:

_____

_____

_____

_____

_____

_____

Key things you've learned through training:

_____

_____

_____

_____

_____

_____

continued on next page

Handout 9–10, continued

Recognizing and Overcoming Communication Challenges

Communication Plusses and Minuses

THINGS TO DO	PITFALLS TO AVOID

What About You?

Ways in which **you** model good team communication:

_____

_____

_____

_____

_____

Ways in which **you** set a bad example of communication for members of your team or group:

_____

_____

_____

_____

_____

_____

Handout 9–11
Effective Communication: The Foundation to Demonstrating Teamwork

Objectives

- Identify listening and speaking behaviors that enhance or hinder teamwork
- Improve skills in listening, sharing ideas, and giving and receiving feedback

Notes—Are You Listening . . . Or Just Waiting to Talk?

SEVEN LISTENING SINS	SEVEN LISTENING VIRTUES
1.	1.
2.	2.
3.	3.
4.	4.
5.	5.
6.	6.
7.	7.

Notes on Nonverbal Communication:

_____

_____

_____

_____

_____

_____

_____

_____

_____

_____

_____

_____

continued on next page

Handout 9–11, continued

Effective Communication: The Foundation to Demonstrating Teamwork

Notes on Improving Messages:

_____

_____

_____

_____

_____

_____

_____

_____

_____

_____

_____

Notes on Email:

_____

_____

_____

_____

_____

_____

_____

_____

_____

_____

_____

_____

_____

Assessments, Tools and Training Instruments

What's in This Chapter?

- Three assessments for use as participant pre-work in preparation for the workshops

- Three tools to assist the instructor in conducting the workshops

- Six training instruments for use by participants in the workshops

This chapter contains the assessments referred to in chapter 3 and in the three workshops that are part of this book. It also contains the various training instruments and tools used throughout the book.

Electronic versions of these materials are located on the CD in the file folders labeled "Assessments," "Instruments," and "Tools." For easy reference, the file naming convention follows the labels used in this book (that is, Assessment 10–1, Instrument 10–2, and so forth).

Assessment 10–1

Organizational Teamwork Assessment

Instructions: Review each statement and select the response that best matches your view of teamwork within your organization. Provide a copy of this tool to the employees who report directly to you and have them complete the assessment. *Assure them that their responses can be anonymous.* For a more complete picture of how employees perceive teamwork throughout the organization, invite a broad array of employees to respond to this assessment rather than only those workers who report to you.

TEAMWORK BEHAVIORS	YES	NO	NOT SURE
1. Employees can articulate company goals.	☐	☐	☐
2. All employees buy into company goals.	☐	☐	☐
3. Managers and team leaders throughout the organization do an excellent job of establishing team or departmental goals that clearly link to company goals.	☐	☐	☐
4. Our organization has clearly defined what the teamwork competencies are and the behaviors that are indicative of teamwork.	☐	☐	☐
5. Our organization has defined why teamwork is important and the business results we expect to see from the use of teamwork.	☐	☐	☐
6. Senior-level managers model teamwork for the rest of the organization.	☐	☐	☐
7. Employees in this organization would describe the organization as having a climate of trust.	☐	☐	☐
8. Collaboration is encouraged as a positive way to accomplish goals; competition among functional areas, departments, and/or teams is minimal.	☐	☐	☐
9. Employees work cooperatively with individuals from other departments or work units when needed to accomplish a goal.	☐	☐	☐
10. Two significant criteria for promotion in this organization are how well an individual works with others and how effectively the individual collaborates to accomplish goals.	☐	☐	☐
11. Rewards and incentives are structured to reward teamwork as much as or more than individual performance or accomplishments.	☐	☐	☐

continued on next page

Assessment 10–1, continued

Organizational Teamwork Assessment

TEAMWORK BEHAVIORS	YES	NO	NOT SURE
12. When teams or departments encounter barriers to completing projects or getting work done, senior management serves as a means for removing these roadblocks.	☐	☐	☐
13. Employees within the organization willingly share their expertise with others to accomplish common goals.	☐	☐	☐
14. Employees routinely share ideas with each other and allow individual ideas to become team or organizational ideas.	☐	☐	☐
15. Communication throughout the organization is excellent.	☐	☐	☐

Collating Team Results

Instructions: Use the table below to tally the number of *yes, no,* and *not sure* responses you and the employees who report to you gave to each of the 15 items. You can then compare your view of the organization's teamwork climate to the views of the others. Their views are probably the more accurate ones, so discrepancies between their responses and yours indicate areas that may need to be addressed.

	YES	NO	NOT SURE
Responses of those who report to me (item #1)	☐	☐	☐
My response (item #1)	☐	☐	☐
Responses of those who report to me (item #2)	☐	☐	☐
My response (item #2)	☐	☐	☐
Responses of those who report to me (item #3)	☐	☐	☐
My response (item #3)	☐	☐	☐
Responses of those who report to me (item #4)	☐	☐	☐
My response (item #4)	☐	☐	☐
Responses of those who report to me (item #5)	☐	☐	☐
My response (item #5)	☐	☐	☐
Responses of those who report to me (item #6)	☐	☐	☐
My response (item #6)	☐	☐	☐

continued on next page

Assessment 10–1, continued
Organizational Teamwork Assessment

	YES	NO	NOT SURE
Responses of those who report to me (item #7)	☐	☐	☐
My response (item #7)	☐	☐	☐
Responses of those who report to me (item #8)	☐	☐	☐
My response (item #8)	☐	☐	☐
Responses of those who report to me (item #9)	☐	☐	☐
My response (item #9)	☐	☐	☐
Responses of those who report to me (item #10)	☐	☐	☐
My response (item #10)	☐	☐	☐
Responses of those who report to me (item #11)	☐	☐	☐
My response (item #11)	☐	☐	☐
Responses of those who report to me (item #12)	☐	☐	☐
My response (item #12)	☐	☐	☐
Responses of those who report to me (item #13)	☐	☐	☐
My response (item #13)	☐	☐	☐
Responses of those who report to me (item #14)	☐	☐	☐
My response (item #14)	☐	☐	☐
Responses of those who report to me (item #15)	☐	☐	☐
My response (item #15)	☐	☐	☐

Assessment 10–2
Is Teamwork Happening Where You Are?

Instructions: Make enough copies of the first page of this tool so you and every member of your team or department can complete this team assessment. Assure your team members that their responses to it are anonymous—you won't try to figure out who said what. After everyone has completed the assessment, use the second page to collate the responses. Bring a copy of the tool and your team results with you to the Fostering Teamwork workshop.

TEAMWORK BEHAVIORS	YES	USUALLY	OCCASIONALLY	NO
1. Every member of my team or group knows the goal(s) we are working toward.	☐			☐
2. All team members buy into team or department goals.	☐			☐
3. Everyone on the team contributes to figuring out the best way(s) to achieve the goal(s).	☐	☐	☐	☐
4. Team members do a good job of listening to each other and responding to each other's ideas in a positive way.	☐	☐	☐	☐
5. Every team member feels comfortable expressing concerns to other team members.	☐	☐	☐	☐
6. When a disagreement occurs, everyone feels comfortable acknowledging it and working to resolve it.	☐	☐	☐	☐
7. Team members willingly assist each other as needed to accomplish work.	☐	☐	☐	☐
8. Team members work cooperatively with people from other departments or work units when needed to accomplish a task.	☐	☐	☐	☐
9. Team members work to create solutions that everyone on the team can support.	☐	☐	☐	☐
10. When consensus is not possible, all team members support the majority decision.	☐	☐	☐	☐
11. Team members are willing to share their professional expertise with each other as part of the effort to accomplish team goals. They do not withhold information or ideas as a way to get ahead themselves.	☐	☐	☐	☐
12. Team members routinely share ideas with each other and allow individual ideas to become team ideas.	☐	☐	☐	☐

continued on next page

Assessment 10–2, continued

Is Teamwork Happening Where You Are?

Collating Team Results

Instructions: Total the number of *yes (Y), usually (U), occasionally (O),* and *no (N)* responses that team members gave to each of the 12 items Mark your response to each item where indicated so you can compare your view of the team with the team members' view of it.

	Y	U	O	N		Y	U	O	N
Team response (item #1)	☐			☐	Team response (item #7)	☐	☐	☐	☐
Your response (item #1)	☐			☐	Your response (item #7)	☐	☐	☐	☐
Team response (item #2)	☐			☐	Team response (item #8)	☐	☐	☐	☐
Your response (item #2)	☐			☐	Your response (item #8)	☐	☐	☐	☐
Team response (item #3)	☐	☐	☐	☐	Team response (item #9)	☐	☐	☐	☐
Your response (item #3)	☐	☐	☐	☐	Your response (item #9)	☐	☐	☐	☐
Team response (item #4)	☐	☐	☐	☐	Team response (item #10)	☐	☐	☐	☐
Your response (item #4)	☐	☐	☐	☐	Your response (item #10)	☐	☐	☐	☐
Team response (item #5)	☐	☐	☐	☐	Team response (item #11)	☐	☐	☐	☐
Your response (item #5)	☐	☐	☐	☐	Your response (item #11)	☐	☐	☐	☐
Team response (item #6)	☐	☐	☐	☐	Team response (item #12)	☐	☐	☐	☐
Your response (item #6)	☐	☐	☐	☐	Your response (item #12)	☐	☐	☐	☐

Assessment 10–3
Am I a Team Player?

Instructions: Complete this self-assessment. No one will see it but you. Bring this tool with you to your upcoming training workshop: Developing Teamwork Skills.

TEAMWORK BEHAVIORS	YES	NO	NOT SURE
1. I clearly understand the goal(s) I'm supporting within my area.	☐	☐	☐
2. Other members of my team or group would describe me as an effective listener who responds constructively to their ideas.	☐	☐	☐
3. Other members of my team or work group would agree that I willingly share my ideas with them.	☐	☐	☐
4. I am comfortable acknowledging conflict when it exists in my team or group.	☐	☐	☐
5. I effectively express disagreement with others, and I am comfortable doing so.	☐	☐	☐
6. I give feedback to other members of my team or group for the purpose of improving the team's or group's dynamics, processes, or outputs.	☐	☐	☐
7. I willingly assist other team members in accomplishing a work task—even when I'm not explicitly told to do so.	☐	☐	☐
8. My colleagues would describe me as a "team player."	☐	☐	☐
9. I routinely look for ways to use collaboration and cooperation as a means to getting things done more efficiently.	☐	☐	☐
10. If asked, my teammates or co-workers would say that I value collaboration and cooperation with others.	☐	☐	☐
11. I believe that my efforts to collaborate and cooperate with others are important to being recognized and rewarded within this company.	☐	☐	☐
12. When solutions to problems are beyond my ability or my team/group's ability, I work actively with other units to resolve the problem.	☐	☐	☐
13. When problems arise or a decision needs to be made, I work toward a solution that all my team members or group members can support.	☐	☐	☐

continued on next page

Assessment 10–3, continued

Am I a Team Player?

TEAMWORK BEHAVIORS	YES	NO	NOT SURE
14. When a majority of my team members support a decision with which I personally do not agree, I am still able to support the team decision.	☐	☐	☐
15. I believe teamwork is important to achieving personal and company goals.	☐	☐	☐

Collating Results

Instructions: Use the table below to tally your results.

ITEM NUMBER	YES	NO	NOT SURE	ITEM NUMBER	YES	NO	NOT SURE	ITEM NUMBER	YES	NO	NOT SURE
1	☐	☐	☐	6	☐	☐	☐	11	☐	☐	☐
2	☐	☐	☐	7	☐	☐	☐	12	☐	☐	☐
3	☐	☐	☐	8	☐	☐	☐	13	☐	☐	☐
4	☐	☐	☐	9	☐	☐	☐	14	☐	☐	☐
5	☐	☐	☐	10	☐	☐	☐	15	☐	☐	☐

Tool 10–1

Email Message to Senior Managers

The following email message can be used to notify senior managers about the upcoming Executive Overview session and to ask that they complete a pre-work assignment. In the message you will find bracketed directions that indicate what company-specific information you need to insert. Remember, this invitation should come from a high-level company sponsor. If that role is held by someone other than you, then your job is to get this sponsor to commit to sending out the email in his or her name.

Email Message

Dear [*insert name*],

You have [*insert number*] employees who will be taking part in a workshop titled *Fostering Teamwork.* Your support of the skills taught in this workshop is critical to your employees' efforts to transfer those skills to their roles as team leaders or department managers.

On [*insert date*], I ask that you attend a 90-minute executive overview of the workshop and of the entire endeavor to enhance teamwork within our organization. In preparation for this session, I am asking you to complete the pre-work assignment that is attached to this email. For the session to be successful, you need to complete the assignment prior to the executive overview. It should take you no more than 10–15 minutes.

I appreciate your support of this endeavor. If you have questions, please feel free to contact me or [*insert facilitator's name*] who will facilitate this overview session.

Regards,

[*insert name of high-level project sponsor*]

Tool 10–2

Email Message to Participants in the Developing Teamwork Skills Workshop

The following email message can be used to notify employees about the upcoming Developing Teamwork Skills workshop and to request that they complete a pre-work assignment. Insert company-specific information as directed in the bracketed areas. Remember, this invitation should come from a high-level company sponsor or the employee's manager. If that role is held by someone other than you, then your job is to get this sponsor or manager to commit to sending out the email in her or his name.

Email Message

Dear [*insert name*],

You are scheduled to participate in the workshop *Developing Teamwork Skills* on [*insert date*]. This workshop is important to both you and our organization because teamwork is an essential competency. This workshop will identify the behaviors that are critical to demonstrating teamwork. It will help you assess your own skills and develop your skills as a team player.

In preparation for this session, I am asking you to complete the pre-work assignment that is attached to this email. For the session to be successful, you need to complete this assignment prior to the training session. It should take you no more than 10–15 minutes.

I am confident you will find value in the workshop, and I look forward to discussing it with you when you've completed it. If you have questions, please feel free to contact me or [*insert facilitator's name*], who will facilitate the workshop.

Regards,

[*insert name of high-level project sponsor or manager*]

Tool 10–3

Program Evaluation and a Sample Instrument

When you first offer a training program, gauging participants' reactions to the training can be important. If you plan to offer the workshop to multiple groups, these data can help you decide if you should expand or contract certain activities, make adjustments in length or timing, or rethink facilitator techniques for delivering the content.

Levels of Evaluation: This end-of-program evaluation *will not* tell you if trainees actually gained knowledge or skill, or whether they will transfer any knowledge or skill gains into the workplace. Becoming familiar with the four levels of evaluation defined by Donald Kirkpatrick will help you understand the limits of end-of-course evaluations. In Kirkpatrick's model, each level of evaluation answers a different question, from simple to more complex:

* *Level I:* Did participants like the training?

* *Level II:* Did participants gain knowledge or skill?

* *Level III:* Did participants transfer the skills learned in the training to their efforts on the job?

* *Level IV:* Did the business see some measurable improvement as a result of the training?

If your organization wants to move beyond Level I training, you can expand your evaluation of the courses in the following ways:

1. Formalize the use of the behavior self-assessment. Compare participants' pretraining and posttraining responses to the assessment. Administer the assessment tool to trainees' team members to find out if they perceive a change in the trainee's behavior following training. This tool can provide you with Level II and Level III data.

2. Find out what performance measures are currently used in the work setting to assess team performance. Compare pretraining and posttraining performance results. The difference revealed in these measures can suggest (although not prove) that training has resulted in improved business performance (Level IV data). Remember, it's extremely challenging to prove that a training intervention, by itself, alters business results unless you can isolate the training intervention from other possible influences (the economy, a new marketing strategy, customer service issues, and so forth).

What follows on the next page is a sample Level I evaluation. Add or change items within each category to fit your organization's needs. Aim to create an evaluation tool that does not exceed two pages (or one page printed front and back). When having trainees rate each item, it is better to use a six-point response scale, as shown on the evaluation. With a five-point scale, many respondents gravitate toward giving 3s to indicate general satisfaction, and this can skew the results when scores are averaged.

continued on next page

Tool 10–3, continued
Program Evaluation and a Sample Instrument

Sample Level I Evaluation Tool

Instructions: Review each statement and circle the appropriate rating number beneath the statement. The rating scale here identifies what each number signifies.

RATING SCALE:

1 = STRONGLY DISAGREE	4 = SLIGHTLY AGREE
2 = DISAGREE	5 = AGREE
3 = SLIGHTLY DISAGREE	6 = STRONGLY AGREE

Logistical and Administrative Topics

1. The pre-session information about the workshop provided useful information on the workshop's learning objectives and outcomes.

    1   2   3   4   5   6

2. The training room was arranged in a way that facilitated my learning.

    1   2   3   4   5   6

3. The location of the workshop, and/or the directions for finding the training location, were clear and easy to follow.

    1   2   3   4   5   6

4. I had the knowledge or skills to effectively participate in this workshop.

    1   2   3   4   5   6

Workshop Content

5. The workshop's learning objectives were clearly defined.

    1   2   3   4   5   6

6. The content and learning activities that were part of this workshop supported the learning objectives.

    1   2   3   4   5   6

7. This workshop was timely and relevant. It dealt with skills that I currently need to do my job.

    1   2   3   4   5   6

continued on next page

Tool 10–3, continued
Program Evaluation and a Sample Instrument

8. This workshop provided useful knowledge and skills that are applicable to my job.

    1   2   3   4   5   6

9. This workshop gave me new information, ideas, methods, and techniques.

    1   2   3   4   5   6

10. This workshop enabled me to achieve the personal learning objectives I had for this topic.

    1   2   3   4   5   6

Workshop Design

11. The participant materials (such as handouts and/or workbooks) were useful.

    1   2   3   4   5   6

12. The participant materials were well organized and easy to follow.

    1   2   3   4   5   6

13. This workshop was delivered in a way that enabled me to learn.

    1   2   3   4   5   6

14. The exercises used during the workshop enhanced my understanding of the skills being taught.

    1   2   3   4   5   6

15. I had enough time to learn and integrate new knowledge and skills.

    1   2   3   4   5   6

16. The workshop content was logically organized.

    1   2   3   4   5   6

17. The learning activities were appropriate for the learning objectives and the topic.

    1   2   3   4   5   6

18. There was a good mix of teaching methods, learning activities, and audiovisuals that enabled me to achieve the course objectives.

    1   2   3   4   5   6

continued on next page

Tool 10–3, *continued*
Program Evaluation and a Sample Instrument

Workshop Instructor

19. The instructor was prepared and organized.

        1   2   3   4   5   6

20. The instructor established good rapport with participants and created a positive learning climate.

        1   2   3   4   5   6

21. The instructor managed activities well, including the setup and debriefing of each activity.

        1   2   3   4   5   6

22. The instructor handled participants' questions effectively and adjusted the program wherever possible to meet participants' needs.

        1   2   3   4   5   6

23. The instructor was effective at facilitating discussion and helping participants bring out key learning points.

        1   2   3   4   5   6

24. The instructor engaged participants and kept us involved in the learning process.

        1   2   3   4   5   6

25. Overall, I was satisfied with the instructor.

        1   2   3   4   5   6

Overall Reaction

26. The pace of this workshop was

_____ too fast   _____ just right   _____ too slow

27. The workshop

_____ exceeded my expectations   _____ met my expectations
_____ was below my expectations

28. My overall rating of this workshop is

_____ very poor   _____ poor   _____ average   _____ above average
_____ excellent

continued on next page

Tool 10–3, continued

Program Evaluation and a Sample Instrument

Comments

What I found most helpful in this workshop was

_____

_____

_____

_____

_____

_____

_____

_____

_____

_____

What I would change is

_____

_____

_____

_____

_____

_____

_____

_____

_____

_____

_____

Training Instrument 10–1

Tower-Building Exercise, Part 1

Instructions:

- ◆ You have seven minutes for this activity.

- ◆ Using only the supplies provided, build the tallest tower you can.

- ◆ Make sure the tower is sturdy enough to stand on its own and support the weight of a candy bar.

- ◆ A prize will go to the <u>team leader</u> whose team builds the tallest tower.

Training Instrument 10–2

Tower-Building Exercise, Part 2

Instructions: Your task remains the same as the first time this exercise was performed. This time, however, see how well you can avoid the pitfalls that may have occurred in the first attempt at this exercise.

◆ You have seven minutes for this activity.

◆ Using only the supplies provided, build the tallest tower you can.

◆ Make sure the tower is sturdy enough to stand on its own and support the weight of a candy bar.

◆ A prize will go to the <u>team</u> that builds the tallest tower.

Training Instrument 10–3

Bridge Building for Fostering Teamwork

Objectives

- Identify and implement an effective communication strategy

- Apply as many behaviors associated with fostering teamwork as possible to complete the team task on time and with the resources allocated

- Overcome real-world challenges to effective communication

Your Team's Assignment

Instructions: You have **45 minutes** to plan and complete the construction of a bridge that will support five pounds and stand at least one foot above the surface on which it's constructed. The bridge must be freestanding—not anchored to a piece of furniture or a wall. It must also be at least two feet in length.

These are your constraints:

- Your team is geographically dispersed. Half of the team is "local" and the other half works in another city (that is, across the room). Each half of the team is responsible for constructing half the bridge. The two halves must then be joined after construction is complete. Geographically dispersed members will not be able to see each other except during face-to-face meetings. During meetings, you may view the other members' construction in the meeting location.

- Your total project cost—for supplies, shipping, telephone calls, travel, and meetings— cannot exceed $10,000. In addition, for every $100 budgeted that you do not spend, you will earn a $100 bonus.

Logistics for Phone Calls, Conference Calls, and Face-to-Face Meetings

Phone calls and conference calls: If one or more team members from one geographic location decide they need to make a phone call to one or more team members in a remote location, they simply call out to the person or people they want to talk with. The members who want to converse then go to the chairs in the middle of the room. These members then conduct the "phone call" or "conference call." Members in the same location may face each other. Members from different locations sit back-to-back.

Face-to-face meetings: Members agree to a common meeting place—either one "geographic" location or the other. All members gather at the agreed location and conduct the meeting. At this time, members may look at the construction occurring at this geographic location.

continued on next page

Training Instrument 10–3, continued

Bridge Building for Fostering Teamwork

Costs

As you make decisions about team communication, task execution, and resources, use the following chart of expenses to guide you:

EXPENSE ITEM	COST
Face-to-face team meeting with entire team—travel expenses, meeting expenses, and so forth *(a meeting cannot last longer than 10 minutes)*	$1,000
Face-to-face meeting with two members of a team from different locations *(a meeting cannot last longer than 10 minutes)*	$500
Conference call with all members of the team *(a call cannot last longer than 10 minutes)*	$250
Phone call to another team member *(a call cannot last longer than 10 minutes)*	$25
Three-inch stack of newspaper	$3,000
Two-inch stack of newspaper	$2,000
Roll of masking tape	$1,000
Shipping of masking tape or supplies to remote location	$250

continued on next page

Observer's Role for Fostering Teamwork Workshop

Instructions: As an observer, your job is to pay attention to the team leader's behavior throughout the simulation. Use the checklist below to record your observations related to the team leader's actions and the team members' reactions and responses. Behaviors to watch for are identified in the left-hand column. Be prepared to share your observations at the end of the simulation. Your role is a critical one because you can remain neutral. Think of yourself as a fly on the wall. Avoid making any comments to the team about what you are observing. Also avoid making any suggestions on how best to complete the task or handle problems that arise during the simulation.

Observation Checklist

LEADER'S BEHAVIOR	WHAT LEADER DID WELL	WHAT LEADER FAILED TO DO	MEMBERS' REACTIONS TO LEADER'S BEHAVIOR
1. Promotes and gains buy-in and agreement on a common mission and goal			
2. Clarifies roles, responsibilities, and accountabilities			
3. Reinforces mission or goal on an ongoing basis			
4. Establishes and implements a communication framework, which may include			

- deciding how often to communicate
- deciding what to communicate
- deciding when to use each method—when to use email, when to use a phone call, and when to have a face-to-face meeting

5. Creates an environment that reinforces teamwork in one or more of the following ways:
   - structures rewards and incentives to reinforce collaboration
   - creates an atmosphere that encourages collaboration instead of competition
   - provides opportunities for people to learn how to work together
   - cultivates trust among team members

6. Recognizes the behaviors that contribute to teamwork; coaches the team and individuals within the team on these behaviors

Training Instrument 10–4
Email Communication

To: _____

CC: _____

Subject: _____

Message: _____

_____

_____

_____

_____

_____

_____

_____

_____

_____

_____

_____

_____

_____

_____

_____

_____

_____

Training Instrument 10–5

Bridge Building for Developing Teamwork Skills

Objectives

- Use as many key behaviors from the Demonstrating Teamwork Competency Model as possible while completing the team task

- Overcome real-world challenges to effective communication

Your Team's Assignment

Instructions: You have **45 minutes** to plan and complete the construction of a bridge that will support five pounds and be at least one foot above the surface on which it's constructed. The bridge must be freestanding—not anchored to a piece of furniture or a wall. The length of the bridge must span at least two feet.

These are your constraints:

- Your team is geographically dispersed. Half of the team is "local" and the other half works in another city (that is, across the room). Each half of the team is responsible for constructing half the bridge. The two halves must then be joined after construction is complete. Geographically dispersed members will not be able to see each other except during face-to-face meetings. They may view construction of the bridge during a face-to-face meeting—but only the half of the bridge that is being constructed at the geographic location where the meeting is held.

- Your total project cost—supplies, shipping, telephone calls, travel, and meetings—cannot exceed $10,000. In addition, for every $100 budgeted that you do not spend, you will earn a $100 bonus.

Logistics for Phone Calls, Conference Calls, and Face-to-Face Meetings

Phone calls and conference calls: If one or more team members from one geographic location decide they need to make a phone call to one or more team members in a remote location, they simply call out to the person or people they want to talk with. The members who want to talk then go to the chairs in the middle of the room. These members then conduct the "phone call" or "conference call." Members in the same location may face each other. Members from different locations sit back-to-back.

Face-to-face meetings: Members agree to a common setting—either of the "geographic" locations where team members are working. All members gather at the chosen location. At this time, members may look at the construction occurring at this geographic location.

continued on next page

Training Instrument 10–5, continued
Bridge Building for Developing Teamwork Skills

Costs

As you make decisions about team communication, task execution, and resources, use the following chart of expenses to guide you:

EXPENSE ITEM	COST
Face-to-face team meeting with entire team—travel expenses, meeting expenses, and so forth *(a meeting cannot last longer than 10 minutes)*	$1,000
Face-to-face meeting with two members of a team from different locations *(a meeting cannot last longer than 10 minutes)*	$500
Conference call with all members of the team *(a call cannot last longer than 10 minutes)*	$250
Phone call to another team member *(a call cannot last longer than 10 minutes)*	$25
Three-inch stack of newspaper	$3,000
Two-inch stack of newspaper	$2,000
Roll of masking tape	$1,000
Shipping of masking tape or supplies to remote location	$250

continued on next page

Training Instrument 10–5, continued

Bridge Building for Developing Teamwork Skills

Observer's Role for Developing Teamwork Skills Workshop

As an observer, your job is to pay attention to team members' behavior throughout the simulation. Use the checklist below to record your observations related to the members' actions, reactions, and responses. Behaviors to watch for are listed in the left-hand column. Be prepared to share your observations at the end of the simulation. Your role is a critical one because you can remain neutral. Think of yourself as a fly on the wall. Avoid making any comments to the team about what you are observing. Also avoid making any suggestions on how best to complete the task or handle problems that arise during the simulation.

As you observe the team's actions, your goal is to focus on how the behavior of an individual affects the entire team or how the behavior of the leader seems to affect the team or individuals within it. Pay attention to the domino effect that behavior can have. For example, if team member Jane ignores team member Dick's ideas, what effects does that action have on (1) Dick as a team member and (2) the behavior of the entire team. It's okay for you to cite people specifically in your observation. This exercise is *not* about protecting people's identities.

Observation Checklist

MEMBERS' BEHAVIOR	WHAT TEAM MEMBERS DID WELL	WHAT TEAM MEMBERS FAILED TO DO
1. Listen and respond constructively to other members' ideas		
2. Share ideas with group (does everyone share ideas or does just one person do so?)		
3. Openly express concerns to team members		

continued on next page

Training Instrument 10–5, continued

Bridge Building for Developing Teamwork Skills

MEMBERS' BEHAVIOR	WHAT TEAM MEMBERS DID WELL	WHAT TEAM MEMBERS FAILED TO DO
4. Acknowledge when conflict exists and express disagreement constructively		
5. Give honest and constructive feedback to others		
6. Provide assistance to other team members		
7. Work toward solutions that all team members can support, and then support team decisions		
8. Share professional expertise with team members		

Training Instrument 10–6

Listening Assessment

Instructions: Respond to each item on the assessment and then calculate your score. Select a person (from work or home) with whom you frequently interact. Complete the assessment a second time, responding to each item the way you believe your selected person would answer *for you.* Again calculate your score.

	1ST TIME		2ND TIME	
	YES	NO	YES	NO
1. I frequently try to listen to multiple conversations at once.	☐	☐	☐	☐
2. I frequently become impatient when people fail to get to the point quickly. I dislike excess information.	☐	☐	☐	☐
3. I sometimes pretend to pay attention to people when, in fact, my mind is on something else.	☐	☐	☐	☐
4. I consider myself to be a good judge of nonverbal messages that are conveyed by body language, facial expression, and voice tone, pitch, and volume.	☐	☐	☐	☐
5. I often interrupt people to ask questions before they have finished what they are saying.	☐	☐	☐	☐
6. To end a conversation that doesn't interest me, I usually divert my attention from the speaker.	☐	☐	☐	☐
7. I frequently let people know how I feel about what they are saying while they are saying it.	☐	☐	☐	☐
8. I usually respond immediately when someone has finished talking.	☐	☐	☐	☐
9. I evaluate what is being said while it is being said.	☐	☐	☐	☐
10. I usually formulate responses while the other person is still talking.	☐	☐	☐	☐
11. *How* things are said is more important to me than *what* is being said.	☐	☐	☐	☐
12. I usually ask people to clarify what they have said rather than guess at the meaning.	☐	☐	☐	☐
13. Most of the time, I make a concerted effort to understand other people's points of view when I disagree.	☐	☐	☐	☐
14. I frequently attempt to envision a conversation before it occurs in an effort to be prepared.	☐	☐	☐	☐
15. Most other people feel I have understood their point of view when we disagree.	☐	☐	☐	☐

continued on next page

Training Instrument 10–6, continued
Listening Assessment

Scoring and Interpreting Both Rounds of the Listening Assessment

ITEM NUMBER	CORRECT ANSWER	EXPLANATION
1	No	Humans have a limited listening capacity. The more conversations you try to listen to at once, the less fully you can listen to each one.
2	No	A *yes* answer shows that you have more concern for speed than for accuracy, depth, and interpretation on the part of the speaker. You are also likely to miss out on nonverbal communication (body language, tone, posture, and so forth).
3	No	You will get caught! When you do, people not only feel angry that you weren't listening, but they also feel deceived. Telling someone up front that you can't listen at this time is the lesser of two evils.
4	Yes	About 70 percent of the meaning of a message is conveyed nonverbally. If you answered *no* to this question, you're missing most of the message.
5	No	A *yes* answer indicates a failure to sequence listening behaviors. You're probably evaluating incomplete information as well as risking alienating the speaker whom you are interrupting.
6	No	Diverting attention is a leave-taking behavior. It's rude, especially because most speakers will realize you are tuning them out.
7	No	Evaluative feedback given during the course of a message leads to potentially changing the message to make it more agreeable (and possibly less accurate or truthful).
8	No	Don't feel compelled to avoid silence. It's important to be thoughtful in your response if the topic is one requiring discussion and decision making.
9	No	You risk missing parts of the message because you aren't waiting to hear all information before making judgments. Wait for full and complete information before you start the evaluation process.
10	No	You can't listen if you are simply waiting to talk.

continued on next page

Training Instrument 10–6, continued

Listening Assessment

ITEM NUMBER	CORRECT ANSWER	EXPLANATION
11	No	Semantics can drive people crazy. Don't get overly concerned with the verbiage. Pay attention to what the speaker is telling you. Don't waste excess time evaluating whether you would have phrased it differently.
12	Yes	Whenever you're in doubt, ask for feedback. Use reflective listening to make sure you understand.
13	Yes	Most of us don't. Instead we focus on getting *our* points of view across.
14	No	A *yes* answer *may* cause you problems because you get tripped up when the conversation doesn't flow the way you envisioned it. You may become defensive as a listener if you do this and the other person doesn't respond as you envisioned.
15	Yes	We should listen for feedback from others that shows their approval of our ability to listen effectively to them.

NUMBER OF ITEMS YOU ANSWERED CORRECTLY	INTERPRETATION OF YOUR SCORE
14–15	You are an excellent listener. People will enjoy talking with you, and you will have excellent credibility as a listener.
12–13	You are a good listener. With minimal effort, you can become an excellent listener.
10–11	You will benefit from improving your skills. Develop an action plan to correct the behaviors that hinder your listening ability.
8–9	Your listening skills need significant development if you are to become effective. Develop an action plan to correct the behaviors that hinder your listening ability.

Creating an Implementation Strategy

- A comprehensive list of steps to take in devising an implementation strategy

- An assessment for determining how ready your organization is to institute a training program

- A template for use in creating an implementation plan

Training can be an event that is quickly delivered and soon forgotten or it can be part of an overall performance improvement strategy. For training to morph from "flavor of the month" into a vital facet of a successful continuous improvement process requires an implementation strategy. This strategy must be more than a logistics schedule. An implementation strategy is a tactical process for achieving a performance improvement goal. If improving teamwork is the goal, then a tactical process must be developed to accomplish this goal.

Successfully implementing any performance improvement strategy requires you to take the following steps:

1.   **Agree on what you need to achieve.** The project sponsor and all stakeholders need to agree on why they want to improve teamwork within the organization.

     - *Be sure to tie the results to business outcomes.* If the results won't improve the business or the business climate, then it will be difficult to convince anyone of the value of what you are doing.

2.   **Name and involve the stakeholders.** This seems elementary, but many organizations fail to identify and consider all the stakeholders. In an endeavor to improve teamwork, the stakeholder group is probably larger than the organization realizes.

◆ *Push back when needed.* Stakeholders may have an unrealistic view of what it will take to accomplish the goal. It's important that whoever occupies the training role provides honest and complete information.

◆ *Be realistic about what's required.* Most initiatives require more work and are more challenging than people first believe.

3. **Be brutally honest about organization/employee capacity for change.** Regardless of how change-savvy people are, they have a finite capacity for the amount of change they can handle at once. If this initiative represents a major cultural shift in the organization, it's important to consider what other major changes the organization is advocating. Too much change at one time places any project at risk.

4. **Identify risks to success.** Most people fail to consider all the risks that can interfere with success. Here is advice for avoiding some pitfalls:

◆ *Don't underestimate employees' abilities or motivation to resist your efforts.* Employees are very wary of flavor-of-the-month initiatives. People who have been with the organization for several years will be able to point to initiatives that got started with a bang and ended with a whimper.

◆ *Don't overestimate people's understanding of the need for the initiative or their ability to learn something new.* You may have a full understanding of the who, what, when, where, and why of the training program, but don't assume that others are clear about this information. The project sponsor and project team will be ahead of the rest of the organization in understanding any change.

◆ *Think of all the ways you can fail.* Failure can come in many forms—failure to communicate, failure to engage employees, failure to roll out the schedule as planned. Consider the most likely sources of failure and figure out how to minimize or eliminate these risks before they can sabotage your efforts.

5. **Enable change/minimize resistance.**

◆ *Provide a compelling what's-in-it-for-me story.* When engaged in any change, people tend to focus on how it will affect them. You must create a compelling explanation that helps people understand the benefits of the planned change or the reasons why the change is required so that they can identify how their situations will be improved.

◆ *Maintain honesty; don't engage in "spin."* Don't lie to people or try to cast a positive slant on a story that is really negative. People will lose trust—one of the essential ingredients in successful teamwork.

◆ *Provide performance support (environment and resources).* Training is never sufficient in helping people learn new behaviors. Think of how many people know they need to lose weight or stop smoking but can't do so. It's hard to change behavior. Organizations that want to change the way their employees operate need to devise ways to support their workers in doing so. Job aids, mentoring, coaching, and frequent follow-ups are realistic ways to support changed and improved performance.

◆ *Reward, or don't expect change.* If there is no incentive (either monetary or intangible) to change, people won't change.

◆ *Remember that transitions are HARD!* Even when a change is positive, people can find it difficult to move from the old way of doing things to the new way of doing them. It's seldom the change itself that people find difficult. It's the actual transition from there to here that challenges people.

6. **Communicate frequently—even to the point of overcommunicating.**

◆ *Share a compelling story about the individual benefits of the proposed change.*

◆ *Convey expectations and requirements.* Let people know what the expectation is and what is required of them to fulfill the expectation.

◆ *Identify the who, what, when, where, why, and how in plain language; avoid emotion-loaded words.*

◆ *Use multiple channels to send communication*—face-to-face meetings, email, phone calls, newsletter articles, and so forth. It takes an average of nine exposures to a marketing message for it to register with people. In an organization where people are constantly bombarded with information, assume that a message needs to be communicated many times in various ways before it registers fully.

◆ *Script messages for managers to deliver;* don't rely on them to craft their own messages if you want to ensure consistency and timeliness of communication. Managers are incredibly busy people. Developing messages for them offers valuable assistance and ensures they send the message that you want sent.

7. **Create a robust schedule with timelines and milestones.**

◆ *Build critical mass quickly.* In any kind of training endeavor, it's important that you quickly reach a significant percentage of the target population to encourage skill transfer and idea acceptance. Thirty percent is a recognized percentage that enables organizations to achieve critical mass.

◆ *Schedule everything*—advance communication, the "event" itself, and all follow-up activities. If it's not on a schedule, it probably will not be done.

◆ *Make coaching part of the schedule!* The activities included in chapter 7 offer four examples of what a manager can do to reinforce and encourage teamwork. Regular discussions on teamwork that occur as part of meetings or one-on-one conversations with employees ensure skill transfer and reinforcement.

The two tools on the following pages—an Implementation Readiness Assessment and a template to use in creating an implementation plan—can help you evaluate your organization's readiness to implement training on teamwork and craft an implementation strategy.

Have your project sponsor and stakeholders complete the readiness assessment and return it to you. If there are more than two or three *no* responses on the returned forms, then halt the project until discrepancies can be resolved. These responses indicate that the organization isn't ready for the training program.

Implementation Readiness Assessment

Instructions: Respond to each of the following items, based on your perceptions.

		YES	NO
1.	Before design or development begins, we rigorously challenge whether we even **need** a training solution.	☐	☐
2.	We identify the stakeholders associated with the project and gain their agreement on the desired performance outcomes the project will help achieve. Outcomes are expressed in terms of changes that will be visible in performance rather than events that will occur (for example, having a training program is *not an outcome;* it's a means to achieving an outcome).	☐	☐
3.	Stakeholders take ownership of the project and hold themselves accountable for its success. They believe in the project and offer visible support.	☐	☐
4.	As part of any training project we do, we develop a formal implementation plan and communication strategy. We view implementation as more than a delivery or rollout schedule.	☐	☐
5.	We avoid making the assumption that just because the stakeholder sees a compelling need to change, everyone else will see that need too.	☐	☐
6.	When we launch a new training program, we provide a clear and compelling explanation of the benefits that individual workers can expect to reap by taking part in the proposed training. We think in terms of their world, not our own. We avoid jargon and "spin."	☐	☐
7.	If a new initiative will result in more work, more stress, and different challenges for the target audience, we don't pretend that it won't.	☐	☐
8.	We identify other initiatives that are occurring that may affect people's ability to handle more change. We consider people's capacity for change when determining the appropriate timing for an initiative.	☐	☐
9.	We carefully think through the impact an initiative will have on how people now do their jobs, *how it will change how they do their jobs,* and how they are likely to react to these changes. We develop transition strategies to help employees manage these changes and to manage reactions to change.	☐	☐

continued on next page

Implementation Readiness Assessment, continued

	YES	NO

10. We identify the **risks of failure** (for example, the reasons an initiative may not work or may fail) and devise strategies for minimizing or eliminating these risks.

11. We view the training event as one piece of a performance improvement intervention rather than as *THE* performance improvement intervention.

12. We identify activities or resources that must occur after training in order to support desired behaviors in the workplace. We outline these activities in detail and develop a calendar of follow-up activities and messages.

13. We recognize that people do what they are rewarded for doing. We hold people accountable for what they learn. Any skill or knowledge that is supposed to transfer to the job is evaluated as part of our organization's performance management process. We reward people for transferring skill and knowledge from the learning environment to the job environment.

14. We have a structured coaching process in place to ensure that employees receive regular and ongoing coaching on the use of the new skill or knowledge.

15. We develop structured coaching guides for managers to use in supporting skills or knowledge transfer.

16. We provide clear instructions to managers and stakeholders on what actions they have to take to support the initiative and ensure its effectiveness.

17. We follow up with stakeholders and managers to ensure that they follow through with their coaching and support efforts.

18. We use pretraining and posttraining assessment tools to encourage participants to evaluate their own learning.

19. We employ performance and knowledge checks throughout a learning experience to ensure that attendees are mastering concepts, terminology, processes, and skills.

20. We evaluate our success in achieving the stakeholder's desired outcome. We hold ourselves accountable for reaching the desired outcome.

Template for Developing an Implementation Plan

This template identifies the information that you should include in an implementation plan.

PART 1. BACKGROUND INFORMATION

Description of effort	
Business outcomes that should result from the effort	
Name of project owner	
Target audience	
Current performance level of the target audience	
Desired performance level of the target audience	

PART 2. RISK ANALYSIS

RISK	STRATEGIES FOR MINIMIZING THE RISK

continued on next page

Template for Developing an Implementation Plan , continued

PART 3. CHANGE MANAGEMENT PLAN

What's going to change?	
Why is it changing?	
How is it changing?	
What is the impact of the change on the target audience?	
What type of resistance is likely to occur?	
How can we minimize resistance and help people make the transition?	

PART 4. COMMUNICATION PLAN

MESSAGE	MESSENGER	CHANNEL	TIMEFRAME	FEEDBACK OPPORTUNITY?
				☐ Yes ☐ No
				☐ Yes ☐ No
				☐ Yes ☐ No
				☐ Yes ☐ No
				☐ Yes ☐ No

continued on next page

Template for Developing an Implementation Plan , continued

PART 5. IMPLEMENTATION SCHEDULE

ACTIVITY	DUE DATE	PERSON ACCOUNTABLE

What to Do Next

- ◆ Decide if your endeavor warrants a full-blown implementation plan. If it does, send the Implementation Readiness Assessment to the project sponsor and stakeholders.

- ◆ Determine how to address and resolve any implementation barriers that are revealed by *no* responses on the assessment.

- ◆ Prepare and obtain approval for your training program implementation plan. (Keep in mind that completing the assessment work outlined in chapter 3 is a critical part of successful implementation.)

♦

Using the Compact Disc

Insert the CD and locate the file *How to Use This CD.doc.*

Contents of the CD

The compact disc that accompanies this workbook on teamwork training contains three types of files. All of the files can be used on a variety of computer platforms.

- **Adobe .pdf documents.** These include assessments, handouts, tools, and training instruments.

- **Microsoft PowerPoint presentations.** These presentations add interest and depth to many of the training activities included in the workbook.

- **Microsoft PowerPoint files of overhead transparency masters.** These files makes it easy to print viewgraphs and handouts in black-and-white rather than using a color copier. They contain only text and line drawings; there are no images to print in grayscale.

Computer Requirements

To read or print the .pdf files on the CD, you must have Adobe Acrobat Reader software installed on your system. The program can be downloaded free of cost from the Adobe Website, *www.adobe.com.*

To use or adapt the contents of the PowerPoint presentation files on the CD, you must have Microsoft PowerPoint software installed on your system. If you simply want to view the PowerPoint documents, you must have an appropriate viewer installed on your system. Microsoft provides various viewers free for downloading from its Website, *www.microsoft.com.*

Printing from the CD

TEXT FILES

You can print the training materials using Adobe Acrobat Reader. Simply open the .pdf file and print as many copies as you need. The following .pdf documents can be directly printed from the CD:

- ◆ Assessment 10–1: Organizational Teamwork Assessment
- ◆ Assessment 10–2: Is Teamwork Happening Where You Are?
- ◆ Assessment 10–3: Am I a Team Player?
- ◆ Handout 9–1: Executive Overview Objectives and Agenda
- ◆ Handout 9–2: Teamwork Competency Models
- ◆ Handout 9–3: Improving the Organizational Climate
- ◆ Handout 9–4: Fostering Teamwork Workshop Objectives and Agenda
- ◆ Handout 9–5: Developing Teamwork Skills Workshop Objectives and Agenda
- ◆ Handout 9–6: Teamwork War Story—A Matter of Trust
- ◆ Handout 9–7: Teamwork War Story—What Really Happened
- ◆ Handout 9–8: Learning Recaps
- ◆ Handout 9–9: Decisions and Other Roadblocks
- ◆ Handout 9–10: Recognizing and Overcoming Communication Challenges
- ◆ Handout 9–11: Effective Communication: The Foundation to Demonstrating Teamwork
- ◆ Tool 10–1: Email Message to Senior Managers
- ◆ Tool 10–2: Email Message to Participants in the Developing Teamwork Skills Workshop
- ◆ Tool 10–3: Program Evaluation and a Sample Instrument
- ◆ Training Instrument 10–1: Tower-Building Exercise, Part 1
- ◆ Training Instrument 10–2: Tower-Building Exercise, Part 2
- ◆ Training Instrument 10–3: Bridge Building for Fostering Teamwork
- ◆ Training Instrument 10–4: Email Communication
- ◆ Training Instrument 10–5: Bridge Building for Developing Teamwork Skills

- Training Instrument 10–6: Listening Assessment
- Implementation Readiness Assessment
- Template for Developing an Implementation Plan

POWERPOINT SLIDES

You can print the presentation slides directly from this CD using Microsoft PowerPoint. Simply open the .ppt files and print as many copies as you need. You can also make handouts of the presentations by printing three "slides" per page. These slides will be in color, with design elements embedded. Power-Point also permits you to print these in grayscale or black-and-white, although printing from the overhead masters file will yield better black-and-white representations. Many trainers who use personal computers to project their presentations bring along viewgraphs just in case there are glitches in the system. The overhead masters can be printed from the PowerPoint .pps files.

Adapting the PowerPoint Slides

You can modify or otherwise customize the slides by opening and editing them in the appropriate application. However, you must denote the original source of the material—it is illegal to pass it off as your own work. You may indicate that a document was adapted from this workbook, written by Sharon Boller and copyrighted by ASTD. The files will open as "Read Only," so before you adapt them you will need to save them onto your hard drive under a different file name.

Showing the PowerPoint Presentations

On the CD, the following PowerPoint presentations are included:

- Developing Teamwork Skills.ppt
- Executive Overview.ppt
- Fostering Teamwork.ppt
- Idea Sharing.ppt.

Having the presentations in .ppt format means that they automatically show full-screen when you double-click on a file name. You also can open Microsoft PowerPoint and launch the presentations from there.

Use the space bar, the enter key, or mouse clicks to advance through a show. Press the backspace key to back up. Use the escape key to abort a presentation.

Table A–1

Navigating Through a PowerPoint Presentation

KEY	POWERPOINT "SHOW" ACTION
Space bar *or* Enter *or* Mouse click	Advance through custom animations embedded in the presentation
Backspace	Back up to the last projected element of the presentation
Escape	Abort the presentation
B *or* b	Blank the screen to black
B *or* b *(repeat)*	Resume the presentation
W *or* w	Blank the screen to white
W *or* w *(repeat)*	Resume the presentation

If you want to blank the screen to black while the group discusses a point, press the B key. Pressing it again restores the show. If you want to blank the screen to a white background, do the same with the W key. Table A–1 summarizes these instructions.

I strongly recommend that trainers practice making presentations with the PowerPoint slides before using them in live training situations. You should be confident that you can cogently expand on the points featured in the presentations and discuss the methods for working through them. If you want to engage your training participants fully (rather than worrying about how to show the next slide), become familiar with this simple technology *before* you need to use it. A good practice is to insert notes into the *Speaker's Notes* feature of the PowerPoint program, print them out, and have them in front of you when you present the slides.

For Further Reading

Avery, Christopher. *Teamwork Is an Individual Skill*. San Francisco: Berrett-Koehler Publishers, 2001.

Hackman, Richard J. *Leading Teams: Setting the Stage for Great Performances*. Boston: Harvard Business School Press, 2002.

Larson, Carl E., and Frank M. LaFasto. *Teamwork: What Must Go Right/What Can Go Wrong*. Newbury Park, CA: Sage Publications, 1989.

MacMillan, Pat. *The Performance Factor: Unlocking the Secrets of Teamwork*. Nashville, TN: Broadman & Holman Publishers, 2001.

Manz, Charles C., Christopher P. Neck, James Macuso, and Karen P. Manz. *For Team Members Only: Making Your Workplace Team Productive and Hassle-Free*. New York: AMACOM, 1997.

Maxwell, John C. *The 17 Essential Qualities of a Team Player*. Nashville, TN: Thomas Nelson, 2002.

Newstrom, John, and Edward Scannell. *The Big Book of Team-Building Games*. New York: McGraw-Hill, 1998.

Smith, Dean. *A Coach's Life*. New York: Random-House, 2002.

About the Author

Sharon Boller is founder and president of Bottom-Line Performance, Inc., an Indianapolis-based consulting firm that specializes in custom training course design and development as well as performance consulting. She has been in the field of training and development for more than 20 years, and has extensive experience in instructional design and performance consulting. Her expertise includes the design and development of instructor-led and Web-based programs, management of diverse teams that blend internal and external team members, and management of virtual teams. Her insights into teamwork are based on real-life experiences leading and working within teams.

Boller has been a featured presenter for the Central Indiana, Western Ohio, and Cincinnati chapters of the ASTD, as well as for numerous international conferences sponsored by the International Society for Performance Improvement (ISPI). She has twice been invited to serve as an encore speaker for ISPI. She holds both undergraduate and master's degrees from Indiana University, and she has served on the board of directors for the Central Indiana chapter of ASTD, most recently in the position of past-president.